On the Edge

A Soul-Stirring Memoir of
Self-Discovery and Spiritual Awakening

Adria Sanders

Sibiu 2025

Copyright © 2025 by Adria Sanders

All rights reserved.

No part of this publication may be reproduced, distributed, or transmitted in any form or by any means, including photocopying, recording, or other electronic or mechanical methods, without the prior written permission of the author, except in the case of brief quotations embodied in critical reviews and certain other noncommercial uses permitted by copyright law.

For permission requests, write to the author at the address below.

For more information on this book, the author, and book-related programs and events, please contact me at info@adria-sanders.com or visit my website: www.adria-sanders.com

ISBN: 978-973-0-42685-4 (E-book)

ISBN: 978-973-0-42684-7 (Paperback)

Publication date: October 2025

Dedication

For my dear mom and my sweet son, Denis...

Dreams are made of golden angel wings.
Despise them, and they will vanish for a while.
Trust in them, and they will transform into wings of your
own.

A.S.

Contents

Thanks		VII
About the Author		IX
Introduction		XI
1.	Confronting the Past	1
2.	One Thousand and One Nights	15
3.	The Beginning: the Witch and the Beach House	28
4.	The Shadow and the Morass	35
5.	A Knife Edge and the Regression	45
6.	New Evidence and Resurrection	65
7.	Telepathy and Keeping the Channel Open	74
8.	Entities and Portals	92
9.	Doubts	133
10.	Lord of Records and Whispers	144

11.	Being a Ball of Light	159
12.	The Bottle and Parallel Universes	176
13.	Premonition, Paranormal Events and Back to My Old Reality	192
14.	Bringing to a Boiling Point	212
15.	Conclusion	224
16.	Appendix: Questions and Answers	235

Thanks

I was accompanied by beautiful and thoughtful people who walked alongside me on this path of self-discovery.

I want to thank my close friend Irina for her dedication in listening to me and for offering thoughtful questions that enriched my memoir.

I am grateful to Alina, who supported my vision and my connection with Rico, offering explanations from the very beginning that helped me understand what was happening.

To my editor, Bruce Hurd—thank you for all our meaningful discussions and for encouraging me to open up more and more.

To Marcus Spray, my proofreading specialist—thank you for being by my side from the very beginning of my journey as an author.

To JD Caron—thank you for your valuable tips on marketing and helping me understand my target audience.

Finally, I want to thank my family:
My mother, for her love and strength.
Denis, my son, who inspires me every day.

My ex-husband, without whom I would never have reached the point of being who I am today,
And my grandmother, who lives on in my heart.

Thank you all.
Adria

About the Author

Me and my son Denis

My pen name is Adria Sanders. I was born in Romania when it was part of the Communist Bloc and I continue to live there. I grew up doing my homework to classical music and listening to my grandmother playing the piano. I learned to love art, music, and storytelling, and in turn, to tell stories myself. I dreamed of becoming a ballerina and following in my mother's footsteps, but although I had a very good musical ear, I lacked the physical condition necessary for performance, so I gave up that dream.

Three generations of women. From left to right: my grandmother, me, and my mother.

Although I struggled to learn to read, once I discovered the beauty of books, I became addicted to them. I started writing in my teenage years, first poetry, then novels. I didn't want to make them public; for me, it was just a way to express myself and feel happy. Many years later, with the experiences I went through starting in 2018 - 2019, my appetite for spirituality emerged as memories of a past life surfaced. I had always been drawn to mysteries and unexplained phenomena, but now my own experience was leading me to a whole new level of interest in this world. Step by step, I decided to embrace what I was experiencing and share it by publishing. In my daily life, I am a pragmatic, analytical businesswoman juggling projects as part of her professional work. I am also a loving mother, a devoted friend, and a soul searching for its purpose.

Adria Sanders
www.adria-sanders.com

Introduction

My pen name is Adria Sanders. I am not a writer in the traditional sense, but rather a storyteller. My stories revolve around my astonishing, real-life experiences that have shaped and transformed my beliefs surrounding the nature of life and the structure of the world we live in.

Once we enter this process of transformation, much of what we think about ourselves or others changes, as we reinvent ourselves with a new understanding of the reality we live in, often accompanied by new behaviors and visions for the future. While we are all unique beings, this spiritual awakening makes us see things in a profoundly different way. What we do with this new discovery is up to each of us. Some choose to share it, while others will prefer to hold it within themselves.

As I have changed through my experiences, I have been surprised by the reactions from friends and acquaintances whom I previously considered uninterested in or perhaps even opposed to exploring their spirituality. However, as they learned more about the nature of their existence in the universe, they have begun sharing their experiences, thoughts, and feelings whose source they could not previously explain. Many have been afraid to share with others in a society where the typical reaction is to judge those who defy conventionality and exclude them if they do not conform to accepted norms.

This has caused me to ask myself: *What is the reason for such powerful societal forces to demand adherence to what are seen as normal beliefs and behaviors?* Isn't the reason simply blind submission to societal rules and standards imposed by others and the subordination of our individual identities in favor of others—regardless of our personal values and beliefs—just to be accepted?

All these admissions from people close to me occurred because I overcame my fears and decided to share my extraordinary experiences through the writing and publication of my first book. Beyond the stories I included in my books, I also shared my spiritual journey and how the book came to be a reality. After publication, I realized my openness inspired the openness of others. I have gained a great deal from their openness as well, finding comfort in knowing that I am not alone on this path. Indeed, more and more people are taking the path of spiritual seeking, searching for answers to questions about other dimensions that transcend what we know. What is this search if not a quest for one's own self?

My third book, *On the Edge*, was born out of a rebellion against conforming to normality in the quest to be accepted by the majority. The book was inspired by my refusal to stay quiet and merely conform and submit to society's accepted norms. It is about my desire to speak about what is often seen as taboo in our lives. In this book, I have found my voice to say who I am. I have been on this spiritual journey for several years and found that this inspirational path has given hope and meaning to my life, leading me away from an existence devoid of color. Without this spiritual journey, I would not have discovered my purpose in this life, and I would have continued living with the conviction that the roles I have occupied in society—mother, wife, daughter, and businesswoman—which I often fulfill automatically, are all that I represent. Since childhood, I have felt that there is something more out there, something hidden that I should uncover, that would reveal the true dimension of the life I live.

On the Edge represents a journey of personal transformation from a reality-based, logical, and skeptical person to someone open to spirituality and the importance of intuition in explaining experiences that, on the surface, may seem unbelievable. Throughout it all, I have sought to analyze all the information I received on this transformative journey from both a logical, data-driven perspective, as well as through the intuition I have developed over the years.

These experiences occurred throughout my life, but I only focused on their presence much later, when I had already reached a critical point. The string of highly unusual manifestations culminated in 2018, a turning point in my personal life, after which I tried to accept the experiences and find ways to understand and explain them. I believe a catalyst was needed for that door to open. That spark turned out to be the sensitivity I had during pregnancy. Initially, I tried to explain my experiences in a logical and testable form as I attempted to maintain control over them. But I eventually reached a point where I was overwhelmed by the amount of information I was receiving and the intensity of emotions that accompanied each experience. It was then that I turned to writing my story as a way to make sense of what had happened to me, and to share my journey with others.

We are all unique, and I do not claim that someone else will experience spiritual awakening in the same way or through the same methods or channels as I have. Based on my experiences, these phenomena that I describe appeared and intensified only at the right time and generally only when I was ready to learn from them. Ignoring them can lead to their disappearance over time and to the closing of doors to understanding the unseen. In conversations with others, I've noticed that their experiences—though often different from mine — also tended to manifest only when the time was right, and when they were truly ready.

Each type of experience I had has at least one chapter dedicated to it, primarily organized by subject matter. Together, we will explore how all these experiences have integrated into my daily reality, balancing business and family life, and what it took to maintain this balance between the two realms.

The first chapters are dedicated to my childhood and adolescence, when my first experiences of déjà vu and lucid dreams occurred. At that age, I found it difficult to express these experiences. Only now, after many years, can I explain them as the first signs of impending changes.

Several chapters are dedicated to how I experienced memories from past lives. I describe how these flashes appeared, how I felt during these experiences, and my ongoing efforts to find evidence supporting the reality of the information I received. For those interested in the story of a past life of mine, you can refer to my first book, *On the Other Side: Memories of a Past Life*, which details how the first memories emerged, how I became aware of this past life story as I accessed it, and how I drew parallels between my past and present lives.

Another chapter is dedicated to how I developed telepathic communication and how I maintain this channel. I will explain how this channel opened, the information exchanged between myself and those I communicated with, and how I have sustained and developed this channel over time.

Through telepathic communication, I became familiar with the concept of portals and astral contact with various non-terrestrial, energetic, or non-energetic entities, which is the subject of another chapter.

A chapter is also dedicated to exploring the Akashic realm and describing how I developed a personal method of communicating with the entity known as the Lord of the Records. For more details on this and other metaphysical concepts, you may refer to the book *Conversation with Xenex*.

Another chapter is dedicated to premonitory dreams and paranormal phenomena. As a result of my experiences, I believe that premonition through dreams is entirely linked to a personal decoding system, and the answers lie within us and no one else.

The final chapter is dedicated to the shift in my personal focus from spirituality to pragmatism and logic, following the news that my son may develop prediabetes—a revelation that had a profound impact on me. The inner duality of feeling trapped in a daily reality—where events seem beyond my control—while simultaneously trying to reclaim my original focus on spiritual exploration despite the challenges, marked a crossroad in my life.

We often live day by day with the impression that life is just about eating the next meal, getting the next raise, or going on the next vacation. When problems surround us, we feel burned out. Part of the reason for this is that we were raised with the belief that we only have one life, and we must make the most of it. But what comes after that life? Everything becomes uncertain, and we're told that some other being will decide whether we go to heaven or hell.

This uncertainty shapes much of our lives. Yet, from time to time, we experience moments that shift our perspective — moments that reveal there is more to the universe than we can explain. These glimpses open new doors of understanding and reshape our hearts and our lives. We realize that we are not merely fragile beings who live and die. We understand that we are eternal souls, and that our lives are lessons—each one a step in the ongoing development of our soul. We exist simply because we are. Even though we catch only glimpses of understanding, when we share our extraordinary experiences, we come to realize that we are not alone.

This book helps us understand this central feature of our existence. As a result, we can approach life from an infinitely more serene and positive perspective.

What I present is not meant as a guide for learning and applying methods to access other planes. Rather, it serves as a starting point for your own personal exploration.

Although my experience is unique, the book can help decode certain experiences and provide answers regarding various mysterious manifestations.

On the Edge was created for anyone who is interested in learning more about the spiritual concepts I present. It is for those familiar with spiritual concepts, those already on the path of spiritual awakening but seeking confirmation, and simply for anyone with a curious mind wanting to understand more about the experiences and concepts discussed in the New Age thought movement. Whether you, the reader, are knowledgeable about these subjects or a relative novice, I invite you to explore uncharted paths and familiarize yourself with a different perspective on higher dimensions, the cosmos, and communication with other planes of existence. I invite you to consider other possibilities for understanding the world we live in.

It may be helpful to think of this book as a friend who opens their heart to you, sharing their fears and vulnerabilities on the journey of self-discovery, as well as the joy, ecstasy, and delight that come from satisfying curiosity and growing through it. This friend is not all-knowing and does not have answers to every question, but can share beliefs and lessons learned, accompanying on the path you choose to take. Consider this book an ongoing journey that offers different perspectives on spiritual awakening and provides comfort on the path you undertake.

Each of us is a spiritual being, and we choose how to feel and how we develop. We each have a personalized spiritual path and steps to take on a journey of self-discovery. One thing is certain: through our earthly struggles, we will continually reinvent ourselves as souls. As we navigate through our fleeting life on Earth, we are profoundly shaped by how we decide to position ourselves and internalize these experiences and insights. Each of us has a mission to raise our level of personal consciousness.

This incredible knowledge I have gained from my experiences is why I feel this book is important. Through what I share, I hope that I connect with readers who have experienced something similar, and those who are eager to know the hidden mysteries behind life. There is so much I have learned that I want to present. My promise to you, the reader of this book, is that I have presented my journey in the clearest way possible, as I share the overwhelming emotions I felt, along with the lingering uncertainties I still have. My hope is that you will have gained a much better understanding of the nature of the universe we live in by the time you finish reading.

I continue to face these experiences as I write this book. They have guided me to become who I am today—a stronger, more confident, and more positive person—and have reminded me that what I represent now is merely a role, a moment in a longer journey. I am just a transient figure, a guest in my own current life. But I find comfort in the knowledge that we are so much more in our brief lifetimes. We are eternal.

Chapter One

Confronting the Past

In front of me, I could see a vision of the man I deeply loved. Albert's face was so close to mine that I could gaze into his deep blue eyes. I touched his lips with my finger, then traced his short beard. A strong sense of happiness pressed on my chest, making it hard to breathe. I shared my feelings with Albert and then burst into tears. I felt that if I didn't express myself, I might explode.

In that moment, tears streamed down the face of my younger self from the past, as well as my current self that was lying in bed with my little boy. I had intended to sleep. Had I dozed off? I asked myself these questions while looking at Albert intently. Seeing him, my partner through so many tragic past lives, made me miss him so much again. It was an emotion I struggled to control.

"Why are you crying, my dear?" Albert, puzzled at my tears, asked me. I could feel him gently caressing my face.

"I am so happy. I didn't know you could feel that. I have not felt it so far," I whispered with a trembling voice.

I, the one lying in bed, who intensely experienced all these past life images while being in the body of another woman, had the ability to record feelings for both of us. As the woman I am now, I had never experienced the happiness of being so deeply in love and feeling love with every fiber of my being. A love that completes a part of me, a missing part in me had just been glued back. I only felt it now in this space with Albert being close to me. I looked at his light blue eyes, and what I felt was overwhelming then and now.

It was the last day in Bucharest, the capital of Romania, for my five-year-old son and me. My son and I had come for a short vacation. On a scorching summer evening in 2024, we were staying in my old apartment, where I had spent over eight years and first tasted the freedom of living on my own in 2012. This apartment held sweet memories, but also the bitter ones of fights with my ex-husband, Haris. It was here that my son Denis played for the first time and took his first steps, and these memories sparked joy within me. My heart ached every time I had to leave for my hometown, where we now lived. It felt as though a part of me was left behind. My son and I had come for a short vacation, and for him to spend time with his father. These moments were always challenging for both Haris and me. Painful past experiences lingered, making it feel like we were walking on thin ice around each other.

My little boy was so tired that he fell asleep at 7:30 PM, which was unusually early for him. The heat made the sheets stick to my skin. At his insistence, I agreed to sleep in the same bed. By 9:00 PM, after answering emails and watching another episode of my favorite series, *Cosmic Disclosure*. I decided to close my eyes too. I knew that we had a long journey back home the next day. Approximately 300 km, it could take us four hours if were lucky and traffic was light, or six hours if not. As soon as I closed my eyes, it was as if a film started to play in front of me. I fell into the past, into the memories of a past life. The visualization began spontaneously. I was familiar with this past life because I had been seeing visions of it for many months. However, there were now new vivid details completing what I knew, and the vision of him was always bittersweet. I had made it a habit to note all my experiences and catalog them by year. While I didn't have a specific goal in mind for doing this, I was probably trying to keep all my experiences in order, thinking they might be useful someday. At that moment, as I lay in bed beside my sleeping son, I was with this man from my past—someone who I loved beyond any other.

Albert spoke to me as he smiled.

"I want you to continue being this happy. We haven't gone anywhere for our honeymoon yet. We'll go to Bath."

Lying in bed, I tried to translate the word, even though I understood its meaning. I visualized some water baths but wasn't sure if he was referring to a place or an activity.

I voluntarily decided to wake up. The feelings inside me were too strong, pressing against my chest. It was a mix of happiness, love, and excitement—almost painful due to their intensity— and I couldn't handle them anymore. I propped myself up on one elbow at the edge of the bed, feeling dizzy. It seemed like I had dozed off, but I remembered everything clearly. What did I know about this life, I wondered? I knew it took place at the beginning of the 19th century. I had been a young servant, saved from a suicide attempt by a nobleman when I was on the verge of ending my life. He offered me a home, and I became his ward. When Albert realized that stronger feelings than friendship had developed between us, he tried to distance himself by arranging for me to marry someone else. My reaction was one of anger, threatening to leave on my own. His fear of losing me brought our true feelings to the surface. We loved each other, and soon we were married, despite an age difference of about twenty years between us.

But what could "Bath" be if he was referring to it as a place? I grabbed my phone and typed in Bath. I immediately saw images of the city in England, which I learned was a UNESCO World Heritage site. I discovered that it was an old city with impressive buildings. As I researched further, I was able to check the clothing I wore back then, and I confirmed that a queen was ruling the British Empire — this was shown to me in one of my dialogues. Once I finished, I could roughly date the period in which I had lived.

I couldn't hold back anymore and burst into tears. I didn't know why I was crying. Maybe because it was a new confirmation for me, and all of this was overwhelming in the end. Was I crying for the happiness I felt with Albert? Or was it simply a nervous release? It wasn't the first time I had accessed a past life, and my first book, *On the Other Side: Memories of a Past Life*, was dedicated to telling the story of my first past life.

Albert was in that life too, but with a different name and appearance. After my first experience with a past life, I recalled fourteen more earthly (terrestrial) past lives and four non-terrestrial ones. These lives varied widely and provoked different responses, and there were a few lives I was more emotionally attached to. The ones I was most drawn to included many visualized details accompanied by strong emotions. This life that I saw that night with Albert was one of them. Previously, I had thought the memories of that life were complete when I learned the important thread of the story up to the moment of my death from pneumonia in my early thirties. I believed the visualizations were finished, and I could move on.

But in 2024, it seemed like I had started that life all over, and new doors to the past had opened. These doors brought new memories and details that completed the stories seen before. As this happened, so many questions came to mind.

What was the reason I kept returning to the past again and again?

Was the past more comfortable for me because I could draw parallels between who I was then and who I had become?

Were there lessons I hadn't yet learned?

Was it unhealthy on my part because it felt safer to stay in the past than to confront future scenarios?

This experience with Albert was one of those moments when accessing memories from a past life stirred a range of emotions, from the despair of not being with my loved one to the gratitude of not being trapped in my present life, a life that was difficult and where I did not have a partner. That experience with Albert was a moment when the past screamed within me, trying to make its presence felt in the present. I realized the reason these memories surfaced was my soul's need to know its past and heal it. I understood the way to heal was through accepting past mistakes and reshaping the behavioral patterns I had used.

In this book, I will discuss a wide variety of metaphysical and spiritual topics, but it all starts with past life experiences. In this chapter, I will guide you through my experience with how past life memories manifest, their dynamics, and how these memories can impact daily life. I have been frequently asked about how it feels to be in touch with my past and who I was previously, with the strong implication that it must have been a lovely experience. On the contrary, my answer is a firm: "No!"

Of course, connecting with our past lives provides the possibility of learning more deeply about how we function at the level of our souls, independent of our own unique personality in each life. I believe every soul has a core set of values and behavior patterns that are unique to it. These will manifest in all lives, regardless of the character of who we are in that life. This represents the matrix of the soul. However, the price for these visions is also high. We generally envision moments that changed the course of our lives and come with a lot of turmoil and painful feelings. After seeing these images, healing is often needed. So, I have also described the methods I used to maintain a balance between the past and the present. I provide important details about how I faced the past life, the research I conducted to uncover it, and how I decided to heal and end the chapter by letting go of my other self. These experiences have played a key role in defining me as the spiritual person I have become over the last few years. Past life memories were the trigger point for a journey that I will describe further.

Two weeks after my past life experience in Bucharest, I was staring at my laptop. In my capacity as a human resources manager at a multinational construction company, I was trying to finish a procedure on dealing with harassment at work that didn't make sense to me. The government had mandated that all non-governmental organizations have a clear procedure for this, which was ironic because public institutions were the first to ignore it in their interactions with people. I knew it didn't make sense for my construction organization either, yet we had to follow the rules to comply with the bureaucracy we were subjected to. I work better with music, so I had YouTube playing while I worked. It was Saturday, usually not a day to work, but I had decided to complete this procedure that I had stubbornly avoided for quite a long time.

I was listening to Abel Korzeniowski's "Charms"—haunting instrumental music by the award-winning movie composer — for the first time, and I felt a kind of vibration in my chest, as if emotions were forming inside me. The melodic line reminded me of the beautiful days I spent with the same previous life partner, whether I called him Albert or by another name.

As I listened, images from that life appeared before my eyes. They were flashes of minor details: a handshake, a smile, the image of a field of blue flowers where we walked, a reproach directed at him, and the way he frowned. These were brief images from various lives, but he was always at the center. I felt happiness and gratitude for each past image, but they also represented a drop of venom I cruelly administered to myself. These were moments I couldn't control. These images, accompanied by emotions, could be triggered by absolutely anything.

The music reminded me of him and how much I missed him and the life I had lived in the past. A past that I only remembered in fragments. Why did it make sense to remember all these numerous past lives? What sense did it make to remember us together when there is no "us" now? Listening to the music was like twisting a knife in my wound, yet I couldn't bring myself to turn it off.

It wasn't as if I was living an unhappy life, either. I was content with my current situation. My life was satisfying—calm and peaceful. I had a good job and a profession I enjoyed. I was part of the middle class in an Eastern Europe country, so I could afford small pleasures. I was happy in our small family, consisting of my mom, Ina, my son, and me. I had no regrets or frustrations about not having a romantic relationship.

However, whenever the door to my past opened, it brought regrets about that past to the surface. And yet, when the past opened up and the memories buzzed, I welcomed the past with my open heart, and I missed it with a deep longing. The past provided me with a sense of purpose in the present—a purpose of testing, learning, and growing as a soul through various experiences. But because of the depth of feeling I experienced, I found it hard for me to find any meaning in my life now. I realized it wasn't enough for me to simply be here, live, and try to change the past patterns that shaped my current behavior. I saw that in the case of past lives, there had to be a reason I lived and remembered them at some point. But what was it now? What was the meaning of me being here in a quiet and gray life without my beloved partner? Was it a lesson for both of us?

In 2020, when I first saw images of my previous life, I was terrified. I feared losing touch with my present self and getting stuck in the beautiful memories without any regrets, ending up trapped there. The emotions I felt from that experience were overwhelming and they reshaped my entire understanding of my current life. As a result, I felt so alone and didn't have the courage or the words to express my feelings to those close to me.

My way of staying afloat was writing. I began keeping a journal, writing down everything I perceived during my past life experiences and verifying the information online. Writing was a form of catharsis for me. It gave me the time to reminisce and accept what I had seen and felt, allowing the emotions attached to these memories to fade away. I healed simply by expressing them. When I noted down what I had envisioned in my journal, I usually recreated the dialogues based on the flow of emotions they stirred in me and specific words that I remembered. I wasn't always sure that the particular words I noted were correct, but I was confident that the essence had been delivered throughout the conversation.

It was like recalling a conversation in fragments and the emotions that were expressed, then recreating it after some time. It was not exactly the same, but the essence of the experience remained. These were memories from previous incarnations, and I didn't always have the ability to fully identify with my previous self and know all the specifics at the time of conversation. In my visualizations, I often found myself in situations where I wasn't sure what the person in front of me was referring to. Many times, the visualizations went beyond just words. Often, words were associated with images and concepts, enriching the information I had at that particular moment.

After the initial shock of those first experiences, and as I started to write to cope with the tumult of emotions I was feeling, curiosity took over. Could I verify all these information-filled images I perceived? Was there a way to be sure that I had actually existed then? So, I started to research general historical information, fashion from times gone by, places I sensed I had been, and events that had taken place.

Each confirmation came as a shock. I discovered so many validations of my visualizations that I couldn't deny what I was seeing. Contrary to being happy that my visions were being confirmed, I wished I hadn't received those confirmations. At least then, I would have known how to treat myself with a diagnosis and proper medication, and it would have all been over. But specialized medical tests confirmed that I was well-anchored in reality. The likely reasons for my visions were disagreements with my husband and the indoor confinement due to the Covid pandemic, suggesting it was just a passing phase.

My third effort involving the visions was to draw a parallel between my past life and my current life to identify the patterns. It was strange how, in my present life, I didn't want to have a baby, thinking I wouldn't be able to raise it. I was never able to put my finger on specific fears—it was a mix of fearing that I might not be a good mother, worries about the costs of raising a child, and other uncertainties. I was afraid to even consider the possibility. When I found out I was pregnant, I was in shock for days. Medical tests conducted before I knew I was pregnant raised suspicions about the baby's health. Because I had a CT and medication for treating my sinusitis before knowing that I was pregnant, the doctor suggested an abortion. I stubbornly opposed it and decided to keep the baby despite all the risks of malformations. I knew somehow it would be fine.

Now, accessing memories of the past, I had the answer. My lack of desire to have a baby, followed by the dread and panic I felt, was rooted in fear from the past. In a past life, I saw how I had been shot while pregnant. I was feeling guilty for not protecting myself and the life I was carrying inside me enough. However, knowing I was dying, I was so exhausted from fighting by the time I was killed, I didn't regret that I was about to die. I was ready to go, even though I was carrying my child. Part of me was also scared about having a baby in the circumstances I was living in. This was most likely a guilt I still felt.

In the summer of 2021, I decided that I had gathered enough information about my past life in Cuba and, using my visualizations I was able to conduct sophisticated research on my existence at the beginning of the 20th century. In the life described in *On the Other Side,* I knew my name was Ani and that I had died in Cuba. Because of incomplete record keeping at that time and a lack of internet resources, I had limited possibilities to find documents proving my existence back then. Furthermore, it was difficult for me, a foreign citizen, to gain access to documents in a country with a closed regime.

So, I focused all my attention on Richard (Rico), my husband from that particular past life. Based on everything I had seen, I created a personal file listing all life details I knew about him through lucid dreams. Armed with patience, I searched for a private investigator based in the UK—because Rico was from there—and handed her the file filled with information I gathered. I told her I was looking for a distant relative, someone I had only limited information about and nothing more. I didn't feel the need to tell her the truth, as I was concerned she would refuse to help me.

Unfortunately, despite her assistance, I didn't find anything relevant in the official records. She requested more information from me about Rico's parents, which was almost impossible for me to provide at that time. I was constrained by the relatively small amount of information I could extract from my visualizations.

I no longer had the financial resources to continue a more detailed investigation, and it seemed the past didn't want to reveal more than it already had. I could assume that the name I remembered wasn't his full name or was a nickname he used during his intelligence missions for the British military. During some heartbreaking dreams, I had seen a portion of his name on a tombstone, which indeed included an unfamiliar name to me, "M...well." It was a mystery to me what it represented. After his sudden suicide in the USA, years after my death, I was not sure if he had been buried in the UK or the USA and this made my attempt harder.

On the other hand, I desperately needed proof that what I had seen was real. I needed certainty that I had existed during that period of time and that nothing I saw was purely an invention of my mind. Having proof of Rico living in the past would have given me the certainty that I did as well. The emotions I felt were evidence, as were the historical or social information that could be verified, but nothing seemed enough to convince me. More questions arose.

Was it possible that I had accessed a vast database through my subconscious and attributed that information as being a past life of mine?

But in that case, how could I have felt such strong emotions?

Or could it all have been an imprint, or ideas from a collective subconscious database? My logical mind encouraged me to consider this version. I felt stuck.

What was my purpose in accessing these memories?

Why were they surfacing only now in my life?

Was the moment of pregnancy a catalyst?

Given my sensitivity, it would have made sense for all this to last only for a short period and then fade away. But just when I thought I would return to a "normal" life and my access to past lives had ended, the memories reappeared, along with their full range of emotions.

Intuitively, my heart knew that everything was as real as it could be. Because of this deep inner knowing, I struggled to deny—with my logical mind—something that felt so evident. I longed for tangible proof. Then, one afternoon, my mother asked me an important question in a low tone.

"Let's suppose you find evidence of Richard's existence. A photograph. A document. Maybe a grave. What will you do then?"

In my mind's eye, I saw myself standing before his grave, which I had seen in a dream. *What will I do?* I thought to myself.

I felt turmoil inside me at the mere thought of standing before his remains.

I replied to my mother with sorrow, "I will most likely cry in front of the grave."

"And then? Will you be able to move on, or will you mourn him for the rest of your life?" My mother was seeking the answer.

I felt as if a train had hit me. In that moment, I realized that if I stood before his grave, I wouldn't have the strength to move on or detach myself from the past. A part of me would remain there with him, in that past life, no matter how much I told myself it had happened a hundred years ago. That was when I made my decision: the past would remain the past, despite all the longing I felt for us and everything we had shared. It was then that I ended my investigations and chose to focus fully on my present life and everything it involved.

Now, in 2025, I realized I was only at the beginning of the journey of discovering myself in different roles. Two years after the initial release of *On the Other Side*, I understand it is not a whole history of that event. There are still occasions when I revisit the past. Spontaneously. Natural and unplanned.

Emotions are no longer as powerful as they once were, yet neither the past nor I have said our goodbyes. There are moments when I struggle to stay present and exist fully in the now, trying not to let my thoughts drift back. I'd like to run away — sometimes from my past lives, sometimes from my current life, or sometimes from the whole confusing situation. However, these occasions of my desire to run away have become increasingly infrequent, and my acceptance of my current life and my adaptability have grown dramatically. I have learned that the past can reveal different facets of myself, and although painful sometimes, I can now live with these images without letting them affect me so intensely.

Chapter Two

One Thousand and One Nights

"Turn off the radio! I just saw two suspicious people by the entrance."

My mother was livid as she shouted at my grandmother. She had just come home from work. I was in the kitchen with my grandmother, who was listening to Radio Free Europe.

I knew then that my mother was referring to the secret police. Both my mother and grandmother were worried. A simple act like my grandmother's could be considered a severe crime against the state, punishable by interrogation and imprisonment. But I accepted it, because this was the world we lived in, and I didn't know any other form of existence. Like in fairy tales, there were bad characters you had to hide from. Safety wasn't something clearly defined; it was constantly shifting, and we had to stay alert to preserve it.

I was born in Romania in the 1980s, during the final years of the communist era in East Europe, where scarcity and fear were the order of the day. While all communist regimes were oppressive and controlling, life in Romania under a tyrant like Nicolae Ceausescu was especially difficult. I remember often standing in endless lines with my mother, not knowing what we were queuing for. "*What are they giving out?*" was the question on everyone's lips.

We stood in line whether it was for sugar, chocolate, toys, or toilet paper. Obtaining any product was a struggle — a fight for survival and to put a little more on the table. I don't remember my family ever complaining about a lack of money. Instead, they always complained about the lack of products. But beyond this constant pressure of scarcity, there was something even worse: fear.

There were other moments of intense fear beyond the one I just described. One night, my mother received a phone call from her manager at work, instructing her and several colleagues to report to the security office. They were all to be interrogated about the disappearance of a rifle. No details were known—everything was secret. I remember the intense horror on my grandmother's face as she protested, not wanting my mother to go. I was helpless and confused, wanting to retreat into my shell where everything was fine and we were all safe. I didn't know how to react, and I just stayed awake until my mother came back.

The story, which could have ended in tragedy, instead turned into a bad joke, highlighting the absurdity of those communist times. In fact, the rifle in question had been used by children at the shooting club and operated with a propeller. It was so old that it couldn't have maimed a chicken. The rifle had simply broken and was thrown away by the teacher, who had forgotten to report it.

To understand who I am, and how I took the tentative steps to familiarize myself with the unknown abilities within me and became a spiritual person, it's important to know where I come from, the values I hold dear, and the people who influenced me the most. In this chapter, I will begin to describe all of that—as well as how I came to experience extraordinary events. My path was long, and many times, I didn't know it existed. In the beginning, even when there were signs of a spiritual awakening, I was very good at ignoring them. Perhaps, as you read this chapter, you might see some of yourself in me.

As I described earlier, fear was omnipresent in every little thing I did as a child. It was a constant companion. To escape it, I took refuge in fairy tales. They defined my childhood. I dreamed that one day, as if by magic, the place where I lived would be transformed. People would smile, there would be roads without potholes, everything would be clean and new, and there would be more than enough for everyone.

My childhood was filled with stories and events that seemed extraordinary to me. As an impressionable child eager to listen, my world floated between the everyday fears and doubts of the communist regime, which haunted me with a constant sense of insecurity, and the enchanted world I imagined thanks to the stories told by my grandmother Olga ("Buni"). She was a gifted storyteller. Often, children from the neighborhood would gather to listen to her tales or real-life stories that seemed like fantasies to us. And I was proud to have such a special grandmother. I felt like the sheikh from *One Thousand and One Nights*, enchanted by each of her stories.

My childhood amusements were limited. On TV, we had only half an hour of cartoons, and at best, they were *Tom and Jerry*. Otherwise, life as a child under seven was spent in the village for those lucky enough to have grandparents in the countryside. If your grandparents lived in the city or were no longer around, you'd spend your days playing ball behind the communist blocks.

I belonged to the latter category. I would play behind the block apartment until late in the evening. Often, a neighbor would storm out to their balcony to yell at us because we had been too noisy during quiet hours. Or we would provoke a neighbor's anger after accidentally hitting a car windshield. You could also hear a child calling for their mother when they were hungry. The mother would appear on the balcony and throw down a sandwich—usually bologna and mustard—that would fly to the hungry child. We ate in groups and shared everything. We traded.

The greatest joy was when one of us had money, and we went to the grocery store on the boulevard to buy candies. I remember a favorite of mine was coffee-flavored *amandines*, which we would crack between our teeth. The coffee powder on top of the candy tasted divine, and we confused it with cocoa powder, which most of us had never tasted. We were all happy. Sometimes, a luckier boy would get his hands on trading cards with cars or football players—cards that came from relatives or friends in Germany. That boy quickly became a VIP in our group. In winter, we would sneak under cars and pull off the icicles, sucking on them with delight as if they were ice cream.

In this atmosphere, stories were in high demand. I would ask my grandmother if all her characters—brave princes and beautiful princesses, dragons, and wizards—really existed. I asked if the world we lived in could be divided into two colors: black and white, just like the story characters. My grandmother sometimes hesitated to answer me.

"You won't find just positive or negative characters in our reality, as you do in the world of stories. Our world is more made up of shades of gray, and you have to decide how much gray to accept in your life. You can't fit someone into a box as if they only have a positive or only a negative character."

But I dreamed of living in a world where barriers were clearly defined in black and white. A place where I could fight witches and, by defeating them, know for sure that what I was doing was good. A world where I, the little brunette girl with short hair and brown eyes, always dressed in shorts, could transform into a blonde, sensitive, and even capricious princess, always protected by a strong male figure, whether a prince or a king. I longed to possess the magic to transform into someone else.

It took me another 15 years to realize that I would never become that princess, neither in terms of my appearance nor my personality. It took me just as long to discover that fighting dragons suited me more than waiting in a tower, counting the days until a prince came to save me.

I was never comfortable with the idea of being a princess who relinquishes all responsibility with the hope that one day a prince will come to save her and take on her burdens. In the absence of such a prince, I didn't seek refuge in the arms of anyone who could offer a semblance of what I was waiting for. There would be no rescue from the castle. Only I could save myself. I had seen enough examples in my life to teach me not to expect anything. Those who had presented themselves as princes, including my father-king, could not, did not know how, or did not want to protect me. It was a harsh lesson for a young dreamer on the brink of youth. I realized I was on my own. And yet, despite this, I intuitively sought something around me that could explain what I was experiencing. I couldn't define it—I just sensed it, and it often made me very sad.

My parents divorced when I was two, so my father was more like a shadow in my childhood. I remember it was a struggle for me to call him on the phone, as my mother insisted, and wish him a happy birthday. He rarely came to see me, only about once a year, and I eagerly awaited his visits. However, each time he came, the energy and positivity I felt would fade. He was a man who behaved very coldly, soberly, and inflexibly, while I needed a lot of warmth. I know he tried hard to take an interest in my little childhood world, but he couldn't. He would grow tired of the experience, and, after a few days, he wanted to leave. He often tried to impose things on me—things that I didn't want or didn't know how to do. This is how I came to hate the French language: through his repeated attempts to teach me and my failure to meet his expectations. In response, I would sulk and retreat into my shell.

He had not had an easy life. He was the son of wealthy, land-owning parents, cold and distant, who had sent him to boarding school at a young age. His family lost everything when the Communist regime confiscated their lands in the 1950s. In his youth, he spoke out against the regime and was denounced, which led to several years of harsh imprisonment. I wonder how much of the man I knew as a child remained from who he was before all that.

I could never fully explain my mother's marriage to my father; they were as different as day and night. My father was sober, introverted, and somewhat cynical, whereas my mother was full of imagination and life, always smiling and with a spirit of adventure. All I ever saw between them were flashes of irritation from my mother's side and a stubborn silence in response from my father. Years later, at the end of my own marriage, Haris and I were mirroring the same pattern of behavior I had witnessed in my parents.

On the other hand, my mother was my star, and I was her biggest fan. Her dream had been to become a ballet dancer, and she managed to practice for a while until an unfortunate meniscus tear forced her to become a ballet teacher instead of a performer. Full of imagination, she was also tasked to choreograph patriotic dances for the Communist Party. You couldn't say no to the Communists, so she was almost always busy. Sometimes she barely made it home before she had to leave again. When she was finally home, I would sneak into the room where she was preparing choreography for new dances, happy just to be with her. Ballet was her life, and she taught up until 2021.

I dreamed of following in her footsteps and becoming a ballet dancer or teacher. However, it was clear that I didn't have the physical abilities to pursue this path—I would have to find my own. Growing up, I felt like I didn't have any of the qualities my parents had. My father worked in customer relations at a Bucharest opera house, and I didn't possess my father's talent for foreign languages. I couldn't play the piano like my grandmother, and I wasn't particularly drawn to books or history. I didn't inherit my mother's talent for ballet either. So, what did I have? Behind all my doubts and insecurities, there were always two women who reinforced the positivity in my life: my mother and my grandmother.

My grandmother's stories faded with her death from a stroke when I was 21. I was left with my mother, who was herself devastated by the loss of the person who had been her mother and who had provided balance, direction, and strength in her life. I have never met a stronger woman than my grandmother. She represented a beacon of hope in everyday life. She was a model of courage and strength, despite the difficulties she endured.

She had lived through a world war and faced down Russian soldiers holding bayonets at her chest as she lifted my mother through a window onto the last train leaving the Soviet-controlled part of Romania where she had lived, leaving behind her entire past. She had dreamed of becoming a writer and opera singer but was forced to become a Russian language teacher. She was the one who told me stories about the Trans-Siberian train and its slow speed, so slow that in some areas of the taiga—the swampy forests of northern Siberia—wolves could climb onto the train and attack passengers. She told me about her father, who had once known the Russian nobility, while studying at the University of St. Petersburg before the revolution—how he would light his cigarette with bundles of rubles.

With her passing, the incredible stories and history of generations of my family faded. And with that, my childhood and innocence ended. Although she was a pragmatic woman with a life tormented by world war and the Communist regime, she told me about synchronicities in her life; strange experiences for which she could not explain. She described paranormal events, like often seeing the ghost of the owner in the house where I had grown up. A house they later decided to sell. There were moments when she was close to death because she dared to contradict one of the Russian soldiers, and yet through a combination of great courage and a sympathetic Russian soldier, she managed to save herself. She left me with a rich oral history of our family, filled with stories of people who endured things that seemed to defy logic and reality itself.

With her disappearance from my life, I ignored these tales. I didn't want to remember the past or her stories. It was too painful because I missed her so much and she represented a pillar of strength and love that had been taken away. I wanted to live in the now, even though the now was a chaotic, unpredictable society following the fall of the Communist bloc in Eastern Europe. This was a period when nothing was certain, not even the Romanian leu in our pockets, which could devalue overnight. A different world was unfolding before us, one unfamiliar to those of us used to the routine and shortages of Communist Romania. Even though there was such uncertainty and change, I saw it was a time to reinvent ourselves and the world around us. I was full of hope for this *now*. It will be different, I told myself, that the beautiful world I hoped for would appear.

Following her passing, I strove to become a pragmatic woman who measures and weighs the things around her, relying only on her five senses and nothing more. A woman who judges the real world as it is, based on what she experiences and not on the unseen legacy my grandmother left me. The rest was the past. The pain I carried from the loss of her had erased all the mystery. The mystery of life and the ability to sense the unseen were her legacy that she left behind.

And I stubbornly denied it as I entered this exciting new existence full of possibilities. I just wanted to succeed in a new, competitive world by being a strong person. I considered that anything unseen would make me vulnerable. Without realizing it, I was transforming myself into a knight—eager to fight life and survive by winning. To do this, I sacrificed my femininity and sensitivity, hiding them beneath a shield of toughness.

After finishing university with a degree in general psychology, I accepted the first job that accepted me. Financially, we were struggling. My mother had just retired and no longer had the hope of teaching as she had wanted to. My grandmother's passing had changed her too. As a child, I knew my mother as an attractive mix of toughness and sensitivity, and she was the decision-maker in the house. But the person behind her, her advisor, was my grandmother. Without her mother, it seemed that all the power within her dissipated, which then passed on to me. Overnight, I became the one making decisions for both of us. I was the queen of the budget and house repairs, and the fairy of household changes. I enjoyed taking on this role, which strengthened me, proving my inner strength that I hadn't known until then.

I remember my grandmother worrying about how I would face life. She saw me as the same timid, introverted, and very sensitive child she knew when I was growing up and wondered how I would cope with everything that lay ahead. She used to tell her neighbor, "How will she succeed in life? She will face hardships, and I don't know how she will handle them when I'm no longer here." I could tell even then that I would be utterly changed by her death.

However, the unseen world was just a step away from me, waiting in a corner for the right moment. At 25 years old, I had a disturbing dream. One in which I was dead. As a ghost, I returned to the house that belonged to me. I was just a shadow made of energy, content with my condition of being detached from my material body. I was free from anything that could hold me back. I was in a state of ecstasy, uninterested in the world left behind. I felt happiness and fulfilment—blissfully from my body and from any struggles with an irrelevant physical reality.

It was then that I saw my husband left behind in this dream (I will call him Rico. He is the same Albert, but from a different past life). I felt his pain radiating in waves, which made me vibrate at a lower frequency than desired. It disturbed the state of ecstasy I wanted to preserve within myself. I wanted to leave him behind as quickly as possible. In that moment, I realized I was affecting him because I was present as an energetic being, a spirit. I was convinced that by removing my energy's presence from near him, I could offer him peace and finally provide him with the tranquility I wished for him.

When I woke up, everything still felt so real to me. It was strange—I hadn't thought about death since my grandmother's passing four years before, and I didn't recognize the place I had visited or the male presence at that time. In hindsight, I now realize this was "Rico" or "Albert" in one of his incarnations. Yet, everything seemed familiar. The lasting effect of this dream was that my fear of death diminished. I understood that I had experienced something beyond my comprehension. I also remembered the popular belief that the more you mourn a deceased person, the more you keep their soul in your presence and prevent it from moving on. It seemed quite similar to what I had experienced.

Shortly after, I had another strange dream. I found myself in a desert like terrain, with flat-roofed houses and dusty streets. I wore a veil that covered my head and partially my mouth. I was a young woman, running towards a house. My parents had sent me to deliver an urgent message. I struggled to open the large carved wooden gate. Inside, there was only a candle barely casting shadows in the corners of the room. A woman screamed, her voice piercing my ears.

"Leave! Leper! There's leprosy here!" I panicked.

In front of me, appeared the face of an old man, ravaged by disease. He grinned—eager to touch me. I stepped back, hitting the wooden door behind me. The man brought his face dangerously close to mine with a grin from another world. I was so scared. I felt there was no escape, and that if he got hold of me, I wouldn't return home. It was then that I felt an arm pulling me through the slightly open door. It was the arm of a man. I was so grateful and knew that once again, this man had saved me. When I woke up, I didn't know who he was. But I knew I knew him. I wished I could remember. I felt as if I loved him to the depths of my soul. It was a deeper feeling than anything I had known related to love. In the dream, I also spoke a language I didn't know—it was Arabic.

I chose to ignore both dreams. Although they were vivid, filling with clear images and emotions that followed me for days, I chose to dismiss them. I labeled them as fantasies, desires, or perhaps images that that my mind had formed into a movie. I also understood that the abundance of male figures I had dreamed of could be explained by the compensatory mechanism I used due to my father's absence in my life. It was an attempt to reassert my logical side and reassure myself that all was well. Still, I had no logical and pragmatic explanation, no matter how much I wanted one.

What I didn't understand then was that the mysterious, incomprehensible world my grandmother spoke of hadn't disappeared. It was still within me and it occasionally reminded me of its existence. It hadn't vanished. It was a hidden world of whispers and symbols that appeared to me step by step. It was a fruit I had refused to bite into again, yet it continued to appear in my life. What I didn't know then was that I was preparing for a confrontation with myself. A confrontation between two parts of me that would transform my own reality.

Chapter Three

The Beginning: the Witch and the Beach House

I was four or five years old when I had a profound dream. I was in a room playing on the honey-colored wooden parquet floor. Shadows formed on the parquet, and when I looked up, I saw they were cast by wooden blinds filtering the sunlight. I could intuit the time of day. It was afternoon, and I felt so happy to be in that place. From time to time, I looked at the floor or the windows and seemed to hear the sea on the other side of the windows. I knew there was a beach just outside, and beyond that, the sea. I wanted to go to the beach, but I knew I wouldn't be allowed. I was just a small girl.

This dream appeared often and the emotional state it provoked within me after waking was one of pure bliss. Just seeing those shadows on the floor seemed to encapsulate the essence of my childhood joy. The disappointment was greater when I woke up. I wasn't there, in that place, and I didn't know how or where I could find it again. I cried desperately, knowing no one could tell me where that place was so I could return. This dream appeared less frequently as I got older, but the emotion it provoked remained intact. The images were vividly colored, and I could describe, in minute details, the space that made me happy. It couldn't be just an illusion or a meaningless dream. For me, that dream, that room I visualized, had one meaning: it was HOME.

From a young age, I felt disconnected from what was happening around me. I felt most comfortable at home, in my room with my familiar toys. Occasionally, neighborhood kids would visit, and that's when I would unleash my creativity. I created elaborate stories and transformed household objects into castles, battlefields, and dragons. I rarely played the role of an actress. Instead, I acted as a director, step by step coordinating the imagined play. I assigned roles to the other children and would make them repeat a scene if it wasn't done well enough. It was the most beautiful game for me.

My mother often tried to get me out of the house for mountain walks or to visit other cities with her for fun. Most of the time, she had to confront my stubborn refusal. I didn't cooperate, as I preferred to stay home in the fairy-tale atmosphere I had created. Just the thought of the outside world caused me fear and anxiety. If I was initially excited, inertia would set in. Strangely, I couldn't then, nor later, attach these fears to anything real or to a specific event. The anxiety, on the other hand, was towards everything around me. I wasn't interested in what was outside the house. Everything seemed gray and devoid of charm. When I became older, I repeatedly asked myself about this state of mind I had.

Is this really my life, or did I end up in the wrong one? It wasn't supposed to be like this. It was supposed to be much more than this.

What "more" meant, I didn't know. Only years later did I begin to understand that something within me was searching for the past. It appeared to be a distant past that I didn't fully remember and didn't understand what it represented. My soul was still tied to a reality that didn't match the one surrounding me. This feeling of belonging to another time and place was so strong that it affected my relationship with what was going on in my world.

I couldn't connect with the places or people around me. I saw them as transient and preferred to wait for the real ones to appear at any moment. Except for my mother and grandmother, everyone else around me seemed to me just passing beings, replacing the real ones. I was convinced that in a second, everything would change, and I would see reality as I knew it should be. It would be the reality I was familiar with, one I would recognize as mine. I felt frustrated because I couldn't answer my own questions, and no one around me could either. Despite my inner turmoil and hopes of finding an explanation, life continued on its path, with nothing changing. As I grew older, that life I was searching for and considered real no longer appeared. On the contrary, my invisible connection to it was disappearing.

From around the age of five, I experienced two recurring dreams.

In the first dream, I was at the beach house, playing on wooden floors. This was the dream I described at the beginning of this chapter.

In the second dream, I saw myself as a child, leaving the apartment building where I lived and heading to the parking lot. From there, I had to walk about 30 meters to the right to go around the building and reach the boulevard. Every time, I headed in that direction. At the corner of the building, where an alley formed between the building and a garden, an old woman always awaited me. Her face was wrinkled, with a hooked nose, and she walked hunched over. I associated her with a witch from the fairy tales who would harm me if I got too close. I felt her presence was malevolent. Her very appearance exuded malice and instilled fear in me. I wanted to move towards the boulevard, but she always stopped me. When I tried to return home from the boulevard, I found her again, blocking my way. There were very few times I managed to get past her.

For years, I dreamt about her and woke up frightened, even though years had passed, and I no longer believed in witches or that an old woman could stop me. I already knew that absolute evil didn't exist in my life, only shades of gray, as my grandmother used to tell me.

During my psychology studies, I realized this evil figure I saw could be an archetypal representation of all my anxieties and fears, nothing more. The old woman likely represented the barrier I had created for myself in my attempt to protect my inner child and to feel at home. The dream became less frequent as I grew older and I better understood the boundaries between dreams and reality. My conclusion was firm: the dream was just a childhood nightmare fueled by archetypal figures and fears.

What I couldn't explain, however, was why this constant fear existed and why I didn't feel safe. Despite my parents' divorce when I was two, the ever-present shortages in the Communist regime, and the constant struggle to achieve a better life, I still perceived my childhood as idyllic. Although I lacked nothing essential, I was in a constant state of fear for my safety.

It wasn't easy to find a logical explanation for the dichotomy of these two dreams. I could speculate that both dreams stemmed from the same desire for safety. In my dream with the beach house, I felt fulfilment and a strong desire to be there. The second dream, featuring the witch, was the mirror opposite of the first one. These two dreams showed me two opposing facets of my emotions: happiness, joy, and excitement on one side, and fear, frustration, and sadness on the other. I was fluctuating between these two states. The only thing I couldn't decipher was the longing for home.

The longing for a place I had never known within my supposed reality was so strong that it consumed me. The memory of this beautifully unknown place from another time stayed with me for days and sometimes caused deep melancholy. I didn't know how to react. I didn't know what specifically attracted me to that place, where it existed, or what I should remember about it.

My views on the nature of reality have evolved to the point where spirituality has become a way of life. I have learned to embrace tolerance and respect for the beliefs and views of those around me. In this context, my acceptance of their opinions is less important. Instead, what truly matters is understanding the new perspectives that others choose to adopt and live by. Lastly, I also believe spirituality involves accepting my experiences, learning from them, and developing my inner self.

However, I wasn't always like this. My spiritual beliefs were somewhat uncertain. I was raised as an Orthodox Christian during communist times, when attending church had to be done quietly, and celebrating Christmas and Easter was challenging. The ruling party often scheduled events on these important dates that we were required to attend. Even though my family practiced our religion, my connection to it was weak. I couldn't understand the complexity of God's logic. I especially wondered why He permitted the fear I sometimes saw in my mother's eyes.

One night, I decided to make a pact with the cosmos to learn more about the visions of the house I frequently dreamed about. My intuition told me that I couldn't make such a pact with the Christian God. The God I knew from Christian norms and traditions was unyielding and inflexible. I didn't believe He would accept my desire to understand what was happening to me. I tried praying, asking for clarity about why the world is the way it is, but I received no answers. So, I decided to take another approach—a pagan one. I felt Christian beliefs couldn't reconcile with making an unorthodox pact involving a sacrificial gesture. I didn't see that I had any other options.

Thus, I decided to make a pact with the cosmos in a very transactional way. I wasn't familiar with pagan beliefs, but I had heard they always involved an exchange. You offered something to receive something else. There was a balance in the universe, or as the old saying goes: "What you give is what you get." I believed I couldn't receive anything without offering an equally significant loss. I wondered what I could sacrifice to find out where that place was—where that house on the beach was? Where was that home for me?

It's hard to understand now how I chose the object of my sacrifice, but I intuitively knew it was as important to me as finding that home. I decided that the object of my sacrifice would be romantic love in this lifetime. I was willing to sacrifice the possibility of finding great love, the one true love that I knew existed for me somewhere in my current reality. But the longing for home was too great. So, I felt if I had to sacrifice something to find this home—I would sacrifice love.

It took me many more years to realize what "home" meant for me. After seeing the first images from the memories of my first past life and how, as Ani, I enjoyed the hot sand while sitting and watching my nanny, Ama, I finally knew where that home was. It was early 19th century Cuba. Though I had suspected the location before, I didn't have certainty until 2018. This was when I understood that I had found the home I had dreamt of and longed for all those years.

I also knew that because of the bargain I had made, I had possibly jeopardized the chance to meet the one who I loved back then, if they were present in my current life. With deep pain, I realized that there is no home without the people you love. I also saw that in my current life, I had people who loved me, just as I did back then. This was a profound revelation. Was it too late to take back my promise made to the cosmos? Was it too late to reinvent my current life based on this realization?

In 2018, I was pregnant with Denis and still married. It was a time of great change in my life, and I didn't know what the future held for me.

Chapter Four

The Shadow and the Morass

The transition from childhood to adolescence was extremely difficult for me. The two pillars of my home, my mother and grandmother, couldn't understand why I was so often sullen. I had been this way in early childhood too, but the feeling had intensified as I began my teenage years. I experienced euphoric moments followed by deep melancholy, often shutting myself off from everyone, even my mother and grandmother, despite their enormous efforts to maintain our emotional connections. Although this state was never long-lasting—it would come and go—but when it appeared, it impacted me deeply.

There were times when I locked myself in my room to suffer alone, to hide from others. But I didn't know what I was suffering from. I only knew it was a longing for something, and from that longing, the suffering was born. I was unhappy, but I couldn't explain what it was that I longed for. Even if I had been open enough to express what

I felt to my family, I still wouldn't have been able to put my state into words.

Puberty and later adolescence highlighted this trait from childhood even more. Sometimes, my grandmother would react with frustration to my strange behavior and say, "She takes after her father. She has his moods too." Her reaction would usually intensify my response, pushing me to retreat even more. The comparison to my father hurt me. I knew how difficult it was to relate to him, and in recent years, we didn't have a lot of contact. I didn't seek him out, and he didn't seek me out either. I built a life in his absence and grown used to the idea that he didn't exist for me, and I couldn't expect anything from him.

At the same time, it was strange because I could be charming and talkative in social settings and with my peers, even becoming popular in high school. But just as often, I would withdraw into myself, and nothing could pull me out of that state. And these states were visible. Most of the time, I tried to hide them when I was around my peers, but it didn't work. I didn't want to lose my popularity—something I never believed I would have in childhood as a grumpy girl. Despite my efforts to hide my nature from others, these states kept occurring. They would appear suddenly and vanish just as quickly.

I had no idea why they were appearing. My moods were fluctuating, which seems quite easy to explain in the case of an adolescent due to hormonal changes. But looking at them now, with my adult eyes, I consider that I lacked the ability to adapt to the life I was experiencing every day. I felt like an outsider, someone who had difficulty mixing with others. My reaction was also a protest, a refusal to adapt.

I didn't want to be there. I wanted to be elsewhere. But what that elsewhere meant was also unclear.

Despite everything, I felt good when I was with my peers. I wanted to get as close to them as possible, to be seen as normal in both behavior and thoughts, to blend in. But it didn't happen often. Whenever their perception of me came up, I heard from them that they thought I was different. I was popular, but that popularity came from my differences, and not from fitting in with them. I faced this perception of being different at every step.

Whatever I said, thought, or even the way I dressed, they saw it as different to them. And I didn't want to be different. In adolescence, being different wasn't cool. As I got older, even though I had friends to go out for a drink or to a club with, nothing seemed to last or take root around me. No matter how much I wanted to have a close and intimate friendship with someone my age, it was doomed to failure. With two exceptions in my life—close friends who didn't live nearby—I couldn't form strong connections. But even these two friends of mine were outsiders because of their nature and way of thinking and acting. While we didn't share all the same perspectives on life, we shared the feeling of being outsiders.

I also sensed a divide between me and others, with me being on one side while they were on the other. I felt the barrier between us. But why? What did it mean? Why couldn't I blend in with others?

Even then, my grandmother tried to encourage me.

"It's good to be different. You'll understand more when you're an adult. That's what makes you unique. You don't follow the herd."

She could sometimes be so blunt. And I wasn't seeking uniqueness, nor could I even intuit what this difference was. I simply labeled myself as a strange person.

The same thing manifested itself in romantic relationships. Promising romantic attempts failed as quickly as they began. The reason was simple. I felt compelled to put on an act, talk about everyday things that uninterested me, laugh at their stupid jokes, and let them believe I was impressed with them. But I wasn't. After the second date, I usually wouldn't answer the phone when they called or would bluntly tell them I was no longer interested.

At the same time, I went on these dates with certain expectations. It was as if I had an unwritten list of requirements that I expected them to meet. I was always searching for something, a certain type of behavior or reaction in my presence. Intuitively, I thought that only in this way would I find the one destined for me. Of course, most of the time, that type of response or behavior wasn't there, and I lost interest quickly. Physically, I knew exactly what I was looking for: a tall man, blond, with blue eyes. Why? I didn't have a clear or reasonable explanation. I hadn't had such a masculine model in my family, nor had I known a man like that.

Due to these searches allied with my high expectations, I entered a few troublesome relationships, believing that the person in front of me was the one I was looking for. If someone displayed even one type of behavior that felt intuitively familiar and comforting, without a clear explanation as to why, I immediately wanted to get to know him better. I refused to accept that the entirety of what was presented before my eyes was far from what I was seeking and that I was impressed solely based on my longing for something I couldn't even identify. In the end, what I initially thought was the ideal I desired turned out to be far from what I actually wanted.

Still, I threw myself blindly into these relationships, refusing to see reality. I did it because that potential partner occasionally offered me the reactions I was waiting for, giving me the impression of depth and a soul connection beyond words. I couldn't pinpoint exactly what behavioral patterns I was looking for in a partner, but nevertheless I found something that seemed to meet my blind expectations. Of course, after a while, these behavioral patterns disappeared, and I'd be left disappointed. My inevitable awakening from that state of blindness was spontaneous, just like the moment I thought I had fallen in love.

It took years to realize that what I wanted didn't exist in any of the relationships I had and that I didn't know if I would ever find what I was looking for. The root cause of this was because I wasn't sure what I was looking for. Eventually, I came to the conclusion that what I wanted was unavailable to me.

However, things have changed. In my sleep over the past few years, I have been accompanied by a shadow that seemed to fulfill all those expectations. I felt its presence upon waking at night. I knew it had been present in my dream, but I didn't know who it was or what it wanted. I just knew it was a "he." The emotion left behind after the unknown contact with him would leave me full of delight and exaltation.

When I woke up, I had moments of pure happiness. I felt loved and protected, as if during sleep I had crossed into another realm, a place where I had been replenished with all the strength and energy I needed to move forward.

This state of happiness lingered for long after. Intuitively, I knew there was someone in the dream, on the other side, providing me with the comfort and love I needed.

At first, I ignored the sensation because I attributed it to being a teenager. But the moments of fulfilment repeated, and I had more mornings where the happiness I felt was complete, representing a moment of perfect joy for me. Unfortunately, these moments were rare, and I couldn't sustain the state of bliss for more than one day. After the feeling departed, I would slip from happiness into total unhappiness. I realized that whatever I felt was fleeting, and that what had made me happy had completely disappeared. Worse, I didn't even know what exactly had made me happy.

I didn't believe these emotions were based on religious ecstasy. I didn't believe in guardian angels. Over time, the foundations of my Christian faith had become quite fragile in my mind and heart. I was bothered by the multitude of religions throughout the world, each imposing different traditions and religious norms, contradicting each other, yet claiming to hold the absolute truth. None of them had the strength to inspire me. Curiously, most religions mentioned angels, but I didn't believe in their presence or in that of spiritual guides.

As a teenager, I was firmly anti-spiritual and anti-religious. Religion and spirituality seemed like a waste of time and energy, with aspects that could be explained by a clear and logical mind. I wanted pragmatic explanations for my experiences, but religion and spirituality only offered tools for belief without clear proof, and I needed evidence. So, I decided not to invest too much time in trying to understand the paths they offered.

At the same time, I was attracted to anything that had a paranormal aspect. These experiences piqued my curiosity. And I knew that the masculine presence I sensed in my dreams wanted to convey something. I believed it was a paranormal event I was experiencing. I was sure of it because it was repetitive and the feeling of the presence in my life was tangible, as if it was physical and I could touch it. The male presence could have been an energetic being or a ghost from a past I couldn't understand. However, I felt that his presence played a role in healing and protecting me in some way. But what did he want? In the dream, I could always sense his presence next to me, but I couldn't see him. It was frustrating. And despite this, I found nothing spiritual in it.

Years passed, and the masculine presence never left me. While it was not a constant presence, it was there often enough that I had grown accustomed to it. It was a feeling that was undeniable. Sometimes I ignored it, but it still offered me moments of complete happiness. So, who was the shadow? Could it have been my grandmother in another form? But why did this presence feel so masculine?

My late grandmother, with whom I shared an inexplicable soul connection to the point of being able to finish each other's sentences, still visited me in my dreams, reassuring me that she was fine. Before she died, she spoke to me in a serious and grave tone.

"If I can, I will appear in your dreams and tell you where and how I am."

She kept her word. In my dreams, she sometimes revealed a realm where she resided, a place where we could meet. It was a road through a forest, at the edge of a lake. The road was busy, with people coming and sitting by the shore until they decided to cross to the other side. Even though there were many people on that road, I never once perceived any commotion or noise. The place was calm and warm, and even though families were parting ways, everything happened naturally and without any trace of sadness or regret, as if they knew they would see each other again soon.

Though I was never able to cross the lake to the other side, the moments spent chatting with her in that place brought me comfort. I knew she was still with me. She could understand my deepest thoughts, guiding and comforting me as I continued the life I was living without her. In my country, it is believed that loved ones who pass away remain with you, even after death.

I also knew the shadow wasn't hers. This shadow had appeared long before her death. I hadn't told her about it either as I felt I couldn't explain something I didn't understand, even to someone understanding like my grandmother.

Despite all this, I recognized I was living with a contradiction. While I felt I was experiencing something paranormal, I wasn't drawn to mysticism and had no intention of taking these sensations too seriously. The shadow was silent. Even if it expressed something during the dream, that message remained locked within the sleep itself, leaving me only fragments of sensation afterward. Yet, I knew the shadow was protecting me, and I could feel it deep inside, even though it didn't claim a place in my life or show its physical appearance in any form, not even in my dreams. Still the shadow was there, and somehow, he was changing me.

Over the years, I did many things I couldn't explain, not understanding why I acted or felt a certain way. Something urged me to behave in a way contrary to my nature. For example, I loved classical music and enjoyed hearing the piano resonate in the house. Although I had no interest in learning to play, I enjoyed the moments when both my mother and grandmother played. The piano was a symbol of the artistic life in our home. It represented who we were—a non-conformist family. With a slightly out-of-tune piano, my grandmother could sing her romances, and every Christmas Eve, we sang carols together.

However, there were moments when the sound of the piano irritated me. At those times, the classical music I loved, whether Chopin or Tchaikovsky, drove me crazy. I wanted to escape it, and if I could, I would have hidden in a corner and cried. The same happened with other things I loved, such as history, books, and nature. I usually enjoyed them immensely up to a point, after which I would reject them with such force that I couldn't stand to be near them for a while. No one understood why I reacted this way or what was wrong with me. I certainly didn't.

I didn't associate my adolescence and later years with the emotional turmoil, the shadow that haunted my dreams, or my occasionally firm refusal to enjoy the things I loved. Nor did I connect any of these experiences with spirituality. It took me years of self-discovery to understand what was influencing me.

I discovered much about these things later in life. I saw that I was influenced by memories from past lives, with all their baggage of happiness and the still-open wounds I hadn't been aware of. Those subconscious memories haunted me, causing sudden shifts in my mindset and emotional state. For example, I learned that my ex-husband from a past life, Rico, was a talented piano player who loved Chopin. The piano music reminded me of him. Without fully realizing it, I found myself both loving and hating these moments, stirring bittersweet memories. Most of the things I loved in my present life made me happy for a while and then strongly unhappy because it was related to a past event or person. Somewhere in my subconscious, my unhealed past was screaming to be taken seriously and listened to.

When the wound from the past was triggered without my awareness, I would flee from the pain I felt and desperately tried to avoid reliving it. I was protecting myself from a past that had ended, while living in the present without being aware of what the past entailed. As a result, I often struggled to find any joy in the present. Yet, all those memories still lingered, somewhere in the DNA of my soul. The consequence was that I couldn't heal something I didn't know about.

On the other hand, I still wondered who the shadow was. Did it have any relevance to the past? It took me more time to understand the complexity of the shadow's existence in my life and its mission. Until I could find out more, I continued to live with the shadow attached to me and the melancholy inherited from my father, trying to fight the demons of the past without knowing their real faces.

Chapter Five

A Knife Edge and the Regression

I understood what sleep deprivation meant and how, in this state, we can no longer be sure where the boundary between reality and dreams lies. A state in which our emotions and perceptions are altered. My perceptions and senses were slowed, and it felt like I was living in a dream state as I went about my daily tasks. But over a year after the birth of my son Denis, I was on the edge of despair. As someone who needs a lot of sleep to function, the lack of rest seriously affected me. I observed myself at night when I woke up, and it felt like I was walking on clouds. Sometimes, I struggled to stay on my feet, as my balance was affected. I wondered how long I could endure this state. A week, a month, or even a year? But the situation persisted, and my son, aged one and a quarter, slept very little. I was as exhausted as I had been in the early days with him. I needed to return to work, not least as it was necessary to find a new sense of purpose. I was at wit's end and I couldn't go on living like that.

It was the peak of the pandemic, May 2020, and I was starting a new job. I was desperate to work and be able to think about more than just my role as a mother. No matter how much I believed I would feel relaxed being away from business and spending time with my little one, I couldn't help but feel suffocated. The repetitive daily tasks of being just a mom and a housewife overwhelmed me, and I was so tired. I felt trapped and it seemed like I couldn't think for myself anymore. I had nowhere to go to find myself again, to find Adria, the person I was before giving birth. I couldn't piece together the multiple parts of myself and give them a shape

Since my son's birth in 2019, he had slept very little, regardless of the time of day or night. He seemed to be constantly searching for something—a restless that kept him awake. In this state, he looked at me with his big gray eyes. I had hoped he would have blue eyes at birth, but it wasn't to be. He was born with eyes of an unusual gray color, with which he took in the world around him with both reproach and attention. It was almost as if he was judging me, or at least that was my perception. And in this search, he always wanted me by his side.

After the first two weeks back from the maternity hospital, I would wake up six or seven times a night just to check if he was ok. Sometimes he made squeaky sounds in his sleep, and I would startle, thinking he wasn't feeling well. During the day, he usually didn't sleep for more than half an hour, and in the evening, it was challenging to put him to bed. He simply didn't want to go to sleep, and I would spend long hours trying to get him down. Even when I took him outside, I envied the mothers whose babies slept peacefully in their strollers. Denis just didn't sleep. And as I was exhausted, I felt like a zombie and struggled to keep going.

Ever since my son's birth in 2019, I had been battling mild depression and episodes of anxiety. I felt constantly torn between competing pressures: caring for my baby, whom I didn't know how to handle, constant calls from my office, occasional neglect from my husband, managing the household, and persistent visions that I believed were past life memories. These demands kept me on edge as I tried to balance all these roles, but I desperately needed some time for myself. Returning to work and being present in a more stable environment seemed like the only solution.

In 2020, before the roads were blocked as an anti-Covid measure, Haris and I decided to leave Bucharest to move temporarily to my hometown. My primary goals were to find a job and put some distance between my husband and me. Being with my mother could help us too. Our marriage was already on the rocks, and I didn't have the strength to find a solution. Our friendship, which had been one of the foundations of our marriage, had been slowly crumbling, but the birth of our son threw us into chaos. We couldn't agree on anything.

It seemed that overnight all our views on life had become irreparably opposed. Our attempts to negotiate always resulted in strong arguments. He accused me of wanting to control what was happening to us and being too pragmatic, while I accused him of lacking logical arguments and being stubborn. His emotions flowed easily, and I couldn't handle them. He got angry, resentful, and frustrated far too quickly. I wanted to run away and close the door behind me. I felt suffocated in his presence. On the other hand, I blamed myself for not thinking about the child's well-being. If I left my husband as I felt compelled to, I would be abandoning my son, and I couldn't do that.

I was usually the one looking for solutions, no matter what problems we were facing. But this time, I gave up being the problem-solving woman. I was just so tired. So, I let things happen, hoping that something, someday, will work out between us. At that point, I needed so much tenderness and care, yet it seemed he had lost the capacity to offer even small gestures towards me. That said, I could understand him too—he no longer recognized me either. I swung between being absent or irritable, mostly due to being constantly exhausted with no end in sight. And then there was the past, which had begun to haunt me.

Starting in 2018, I began experiencing flashes. They were déjà vu sensations, images of places and people I didn't know that appeared in my mind. They felt like sensory imprints, each one causing confusion. Every time, I tried to check my memory to see if I had seen these images in a movie or if they were just my imagination. However, once I saw them, I knew I recognized them, as if I had known them for a long time. It was like they were trying to remind me of something. The visions appeared out of nowhere, without any explanation.

One day, a strange name with an exotic, unfamiliar resonance, "Ama", lingered in my mind. For a while, I thought I had invented the name. However, after a brief internet search, I discovered it had African origins, and it even had a specific meaning. I could see Ama in my mind's eye. She was plump, with quite a few extra pounds, perfect white teeth, always wearing a scarf wrapped several times around her head, and grumbled whenever I did something forbidden. I knew our relationship had been very close, and she had cared for me as if she had been my mother. I soon concluded that she had most likely been my African nanny.

Then I recalled a car journey along a dusty road, where I could smell the dry grass. How I missed that scent. Researching, I discovered that there was an area in the USA near the Mexican border that closely resembled the image I saw. How could I remember something I hadn't experienced? I longed for the hot afternoons and the strong yellow light that enveloped everything in that sunny land. I knew that in those afternoons, I would sit nestled in a rocking chair, watching the road to the city. Again, I had never experienced a rocking chair, nor had I ever sat in one in my entire life.

Over time, these flashes began to appear even more frequently. I was intrigued by what I saw, yet also a bit puzzled. So, I ended up telling one of my friends, Alina, about what I was experiencing and how I didn't know how to react to these images that seemed like memories. Her response was brief:

"They are memories of a past life. It's extraordinary! Try to write down all these experiences. Who knows what else might appear, and maybe you'll manage to create connections with your present life."

Alina was one of my spiritual friends, and even though spiritual topics didn't resonate with me, she was the only one who I sought for comfort and advice. I sensed that I was at risk of being misunderstood by others.

But what had been fun and amusing up to a point started to become burdensome. After the flashbacks appeared, feelings followed. At first, there was a longing for a place that felt like home and for the people who were in my past life. I harbored a lot of love for all these memories that were reappearing.

Then, frustration and resentment took over for not realizing what had been happening to me since childhood. I pitied myself for the frustration I had endured during all those blind searches to find an explanation.

I longed for the older man in the vision—the one with the short beard and slightly graying, yet still blond hair. I missed him dearly, and realized he was my father from another time. I knew that this man was one of the people I had loved immensely. I also missed Ama, my nanny, and our beach home facing the sea. This continued until one day, the same friend gave me some wise advice.

"You are in a state of increasing restlessness. Why don't you try a past life regression? Try one of Brian Weiss's videos."

At that point, I didn't know who Brian Weiss was, and the idea of hypnosis made me smile as a response to my experiences. I was familiar with hypnosis from the training I'd done in behavioral therapy during my university studies. However, my logical mind had great doubts about the effectiveness of the method in accessing possible memories from other lives. Still, I was prepared to try anything. After reading some of Brian Weiss's materials and watching a few of his videos, I decided to give it a chance.

I was pregnant at the time, and I didn't realize the risk of facing something completely unknown in my delicate state. However, I plunged headfirst, a behavior I occasionally exhibited and couldn't control. As a child, I had been a cautious person, but as I grew older, I began to throw caution to the wind, taking more risks without restraint. In that moment, I felt the same urge to plunge ahead.

I started the hypnosis video and placed my phone beside me on the bed. It was enough to listen to the verbal instructions. Lying on the bed, I closed my eyes, relaxed, and listened to the warm and soothing voice. I had no idea what the experience would be like. The feeling was strange. I felt myself descending through a tunnel and stopping for a moment in an undefinable place. When things became clearer, I perceived myself as a newborn baby.

I was cold and scared, and the light fixed above me was blinding. In one corner, I noticed a small window placed high on the wall. I lingered on that image for a while. I could feel the cold, I was disoriented, and I even sensed my mother's emotion, who was unsure if she had done the right thing by bringing me into the world. She hesitated, and I hesitated with her. But then I slipped further down the tunnel.

This time, I was on a beach playing in the sand. The sand was cream-colored and somewhat sticky. I was in the body of a little girl wearing a red dress with white polka dots. In that moment, I fully became the girl. I clearly felt her body and what I experienced through it, but part of me was still with my present self, the mature, pregnant woman lying in bed undergoing the regression. I was both of them, yet not fully existing in either body. It was a split.

I then looked at my long, chocolate-colored child arms and realized that I was most likely mixed-race or Latino American. I was so happy just to exist and play on the beach by the sea. I knew this place was somewhere in Central or South America. Behind me, about fifty meters away, was my house.

Suddenly, I heard someone calling me. It was Ama, my African nanny. As soon as I raised my eyes, I knew who she was and why she was coming to me. The longer I stayed in the girl's body, the more I identified with her. Ama scolded me for dirtying my dress, telling me that my father would be home soon and wanted to find a young lady, not a stray child. I knew Ama got upset easily, and I loved her for her fiery nature. She was the only mother I had known. As the regression session progressed, the image began to fade because I felt the urge to leave that place. I missed them so much— Ama and my father—that I knew I wouldn't be able to stay in that place without feeling compelled to remain there forever.

With my conscious mind still in the body of the mature woman who was me, I decided to wake up from my session. I jolted and returned to my room, opening my eyes. Now I had an explanation for where "HOME" was. It was Cuba. I realized that was the place I had dreamed of and longed for so many nights and days throughout my childhood. The thought of discovering something I had desired for so long shocked me and filled me with bliss. Why now? I believe it was because my pregnancy made me more attuned to my emotional side and heightened my intuition, while I was less concerned with pragmatism. It was as if all this information had been patiently waiting for the right moment to reveal itself.

After giving birth in 2019, these flashbacks disappeared for a while. The exhaustion was so great that I couldn't focus on anything other than survival. I was constantly tired and struggling with undiagnosed postpartum depression.

But after a few months, they returned, especially when I lay in bed and tried to sleep. It was like my personal entertainment, except it became a burdensome one. I struggled so much as the emotions associated with this past life hadn't disappeared, and each time they became harder for me to handle. While I was immersed in those images of the past, I felt happiness.

Then, waking from that state back to my daily life, I was hit by the despair of losing a part of myself I felt strong emotions for the people I saw in those flashes of a past life — feelings so intense that I longed to return again and again. Among them, one constant presence stood out — a man, though I could never see his face clearly. Yet, I instinctively knew who he was: my life partner, the man I loved, gradually revealing himself to me, step by step. My feeling was that I belonged to him entirely. It was as if I were under his influence, whether he was present or absent in what I saw. He existed with me and within me, without me knowing almost anything about him.

Then, in lucid dreams, flashes of information would appear, not just images. I knew more about him. I learned he was from the United Kingdom, and I noticed a few physical details like blond hair and dark blue eyes. He had a military occupation, but even with this information, his face was still unclear. I wondered then, could he be the shadow? The shadow that followed me in my dreams? When I finally managed to discern his face, the past life memories began to unfold rapidly. I soon knew I had answered another question that had lingered within me for a long time. I knew that he was the SHADOW.

He was the shadow I had been confronting all this time. The emotions I felt in his presence were the same as those that followed me after waking up from dreams where the shadow was present. It was more than just a feeling of love; it was a sense of belonging, almost as if I could sense his imprint of energy. I eventually became aware that the shadow, Albert, or Rico, were manifestations of the same soul in different bodies and past lives.

Following this revelation, I couldn't believe what I had just experienced. I entered a state of excitement, exhilaration, and happiness—all positive emotions. At the same time, the longing for that place and the people I had seen became overwhelming. This desire did not diminish over time; on the contrary, it intensified with each day from 2019 to 2021. Through the flashes, the identity of the girl, Ani, began to take shape. She became a strong, public proponent for freedom of speech in Cuba.

The turmoil of the memories from my past life and accessing new memories from other lives gradually brought me to the end of my patience and strength by the spring of 2020. I continued to live between two worlds: one that began when I laid my head on the pillow at night and accessed my past, and the other—my daily life—where I was focused on my reality in the present. In my current life, I was about to start a new job in a completely different location, and I needed to balance the roles of businessperson and mother. I had changed both my home and lifestyle, while my little one was becoming more independent yet needed more attention from me.

My husband and I had reached the point where we were just parents and nothing more. I had tried to discuss my perceptions and visualizations with him, and at first, he was intrigued. Although he wasn't necessarily a spiritual person, he was inclined to believe in the possibility of past lives because he too had some inexplicable memories related to the war in Vietnam. I approached the subject with a lot of diplomacy because, even though it was a story from the past, I had existed and loved another man. The feeling that I still belonged to that man remained, even after the night visualizations disappeared. The presence of this man was more real than anything, as was the emotion I felt for him. It was a deep love and longing that ached in my heart every time I accessed the past.

I now understood that he was a shadow from the past, but through my relationship with him, discovered through my visions, I finally grasped so much about what it means to love and how to express it. I also realized that what I had been looking for in my relationships as a teenager and young adult was something similar to what I had with that man. His presence changed my accumulated perceptions about love, and I knew I had never experienced such feelings before.

I also knew that Haris, my husband, bore no resemblance to that man from the past. This realization led to my knowing that I could feel greater love for Rico than I had felt in my entire life. With Rico, I felt I could love completely, devoid of barriers and pragmatic expectations. This realization shattered all my beliefs about love, and it opened my eyes further regarding my current relationship with my husband.

I realized I had made a mistake. I knew that both my husband and I deserved more in life. We needed to give and to feel love for another, yet neither of us was going to find that with each other. We were falling apart, and nothing was making sense anymore. We were irrevocably losing everything that had brought us together. What we had was just a pale copy of the reality I had discovered with Rico. I didn't see any way forward with the two of us as a couple. In 2022, we came to the decision to end our marriage.

Looking back on this time in my life, I now believe that when I decided to share my visions with Haris, I was seeking his support to prevent myself from being carried away by the past. I clung to my pragmatic side to avoid losing control over my quickly unraveling life. I hoped my husband would show an interest in knowing me more deeply, seeing me as someone beyond the image of the businesswoman who loved control and solved problems regardless of their severity.

However, I recognized I didn't have the tools or the support to resolve this on my own. Talking about this with Haris was my way of crying out for help. I also hoped that sharing my experiences with him might help us reconnect as a couple. After all, I understood the past was the past and I needed to live fully in the present—for my well-being and the well-being of my family. But somewhere along the way, my husband lost interest, or perhaps jealousy reared its head. The closeness between us that came from me sharing my experiences didn't last long, and I once again found myself alone with my feelings.

On the other hand, with each new visualization, I learned more about what it meant to love and to feel loved. It was a form of love I hadn't experienced in my present life. Understanding the past gave me the courage to face the present. The images of the past helped me begin to understand my passions and highlighted the things I disliked. I came to appreciate the reasons for my behaviors and the quirks I hadn't been able to explain in my present life.

There were small things, like my attraction to Latin music and my passion for dance, my stubbornness and desire for independence, and my attraction to various emotional and physical risks, such as exploring dangerous places or expressing opinions that were risky to share with people.

I also acknowledged the possibility that I might be projecting everything undesirable in my present life onto the memories of my past life. Still, I received so much information about the past, and many of these details provided such convincing explanations for how I functioned as a human being. I could have chosen to ignore it, but I no longer wanted to follow the path of avoidance, and the truth was, I couldn't.

One spring morning in 2020, as I looked with melancholy out the window of my apartment at the usually lively boulevard, I glanced down at my arms. For a second, I stared at them in amazement and was shocked.

"These are not my arms. My arms are much thinner, and my skin is much darker."

I momentarily panicked, feeling like I was in a body that didn't belong to me. Then I realized where I was and who I was. I shared this experience with my mother. I was scared. I realized that I had reached a point where I needed to take everything happening to me seriously. She looked at me with concern.

"You need to write to get it out of you. Write everything. And no, I don't think there's anything wrong with you mentally. During the day, you're the girl I know. But to put your mind at ease, consult a therapist."

So, I decided to talk with one of my friends who was a therapist and tell her everything. She reassured me, saying that I showed no signs of developing a psychosis or any mental issues, even though what I was describing seemed fantastical. But that wasn't enough for me. I wanted to test and verify my mental clarity with as many specialists as possible. I felt like I was on the edge between my reality and the dream world, between the past and present, between myself, Adria, and my old roles and characters.

It was then that I started my new job, and I was thrilled. I felt functional and grounded in reality again. There were occasions when I had to go to the office, and it was simply a pleasure to drive for the five minutes it took to get from home to the office. The streets were empty, and I could observe nature more than ever. I also decided to enroll Denis in kindergarten in the fall to reduce the stress of all of us being cooped up in a house with limited opportunities to go out.

My son was also at the age where he needed social interaction, despite the risks posed by COVID-19. I didn't know how long the pandemic would last or whether it would become a way of life where we just had to survive. I didn't want our lives to be defined by fear, anxiety, and panic. Instead, I chose to adapt to the new existence, despite the risks involved. After so many years marked by fear and worry, I wanted to live differently.

I had seen in those past life memories how I had died at thirty. Mine was a short life, but one that had been lived intensely. Now, I felt that I had lived too little of my current life. Indeed, in my present life, I had only recently rediscovered myself and started to test life. I was just 30, the same age when Ani died in the past life. However, I still continued to worry about every step I took. Was it fear transferring from one life to another? Or perhaps a fear of death? I didn't know.

In the summer of 2020, the pandemic seemed easier to bear. The number of COVID-19 cases had decreased, and we decided to go on a vacation to the Apuseni Mountains. My goal was to repair the relationship with my husband and perhaps gain clarity by distancing myself from the past through a change of location. I hoped that the flow of memories would cease. The vacation turned out to be uneventful. I had no past life visions and no other memories came to me. However, things didn't change in my marriage. Before leaving, I contacted our former couple's therapist as I knew she had trained in past life regression hypnosis. She was interested in this subject because she also experienced memories from the past. She agreed to meet in the fall of 2020.

When we started the sessions, I told her about my experiences and the emotions I felt when I saw my arms and didn't recognize them. She spoke to me about the need to detach from the past life and the necessity of healing what I had lived through. She assured me that I was functioning normally but also warned me that if I clung too much to the past, I could develop a psychosis.

I wondered to myself, *how can I separate from the past if that past has defined me?*

With each encounter, I discovered how I could draw parallels between who I once was and who I had become, such as fears from the past that had crossed the boundary of time. I was fascinated by discovering myself and understanding how my past lives affected me in the present. But I also missed who I had been. I missed my family from my past life. I wondered how much longer I could go on with this feeling of longing. I felt like I would not be able to endure it any longer. I fantasized that if something sudden happened to me and I died, it would be a relief, because this terrible longing for who I was would disappear. However, every time I finished that thought, the image of my little boy appeared. He was what anchored me in the present. I had to be there for him at all costs—I had to live in the HERE and NOW.

So, I decided to continue with the therapy sessions and heal what could be healed from the past. During hypnosis, I abruptly entered my past life, which I had accessed many times. I found myself experiencing a delicate and traumatic moment—a rape I had endured as a child in that life. Although I had seen those images more than once, and I believed I had released all the traumatic emotions over time, they impacted me again during this hypnosis. My senses and emotions were overwhelmed. The touches and especially the horror of being alone and having no escape from that man's arms was suffocating. I felt completely absorbed in my former 10- or 11-year-old body and couldn't detach from that past shell.

I listened to my therapist as if I were in a dream, and she insisted I leave that body and view the scene from a distance, outside my former body. But I decided to stay in the body and relive that moment with all the weight I felt. I felt it was important for me to relive the traumatic experience to find the strength I needed to separate myself from that past. Only after experiencing this traumatic moment, did I decide to separate from the body and burn all the emotions I had felt. With the help of the therapist, I was able to dissolve any past or present connection with that man.

That man who raped me in my past life was my father's best friend in that life. In my present life, I suffered an attempted rape at the similar age of 11. That man's soul from the past was also in my present life. I began to realize that I had involved myself in a toxic relationship that I had mistaken for love, which, in hindsight, I sensed was with him. So, in my regression session, I gave these traumatic thoughts and emotions a material form. I chose a virtual object and decided to set it on fire, burning the connection with that man and all the suffering felt. I felt relieved.

After I detached from this episode, the therapist insisted that I move on to another important moment in my healing process. During hypnosis, I accessed the moment of my death by shooting. As I fell to my knees, unaware of why I could no longer stand, the idea of death was not present in my mind. Only when I saw the blood flowing from my stomach did I realize it was probably the end. The present-day me watched through the body of my past self, paying attention to every detail and emotion felt.

I felt liberated from all the turmoil of the life I had lived and did not regret leaving. It was freedom I could claim. It was liberation. Then, in my final moments, as I saw my beloved husband, Rico, and realized the pain he was experiencing, regret filled me. I remembered then that I was pregnant and that I would not be able to give life to the fetus growing inside me. I realized I would not be able to be with the life partner I loved so much. I did not regret leaving this life, but in my final moments, I reproached myself for abandoning them so easily. I accused myself of negligence and wished that the unborn soul would forgive me for not being able to give it life.

During the regression, I began to cry for the past. I cried intensely and inconsolably. At that moment, the therapist wanted to initiate healing by saying goodbye to the soul of the unborn child. For the first time, I felt the weight I carried from that life into my present one. It was as if a millstone was lifted from my soul. In an instant, I realized why I had been so stressed in this life about my pregnancy and the health of my fetus, and later, the health of my little boy. I had been vigilant about his every breath, because of a guilt I had carried with me in unknown ways for almost 100 years.

As the session neared its end, the time came to say goodbye to my past life partner, but I couldn't bring myself to do it. I firmly refused. I wanted the shadow that had followed me my entire life to stay with me. I wasn't sure I wanted to totally break the bridge between me and the past. I was not ready to give up on him. I refused to let go of all the powerful feelings I had for him and the way they made me feel alive—giving me a profound sense of being.

I felt that if I did that, it would be as if I were giving up a part of myself. Somewhere inside, I knew our journey together wasn't over, and there were still doors I hadn't opened, places that needed to be explored. Somehow, I understood there could be no separation between us. It was more than just a past life lived together and a great love. After the regression hypnosis ended, the therapist warned me that if I couldn't completely let go of the past, it might continue to haunt me. But I felt as light as a feather and was willing to take the risk.

Now, after four years, it remains a mystery to me how I, or anyone, could relive what was just a memory from a past that ended more than 100 years ago so intensely. How was it possible that I could experience such vivid colors and powerful emotions? How could I remember in detail my life back then, such as where I was, and the situation I was in? After all these past memories, I visualized other memories and forms of the past: the horrors, the crimes, and the passions I felt. Rico and I had always been together, with him as a man and me as a woman each time. At some point in our lives, we would always find each other and become a couple, formally or informally. Later, problems and external pressure would intervene, eventually leading us to a tragic end. His presence was the connection between all these memories.

He appeared to me in various forms and faces. If in one life he was an English nobleman, in others he was Alfred, a young orphan, or Istvan, a country teacher, or even Matias, a prince and illegitimate child. I had not lived any of these lives without him. Out of 15 human lives I have explored, we have been together in 14 of them. In the 15th, I died too young to have the possibility of meeting him. Our joined existence became consistent from the moment we met, and our lives seemed to become meaningful from that point forward.

I had so many questions. Where did this strong connection between us come from and why? Why does he not exist in my present life? I was tempted to explain his absence through the bargain I had made years ago. Was it the price I paid to become familiar with a part of my past as a soul? Is this why he apparently could not exist in my present life? My mind spoke of simple coincidences that I tried to explain through supernatural causes. However, so many things I experienced could not be explained using reason or logic that I barely felt sure of anything.

As time passed, I was willing to accept the idea of reincarnation, the ability to view and feel myself in past lives, and the presence of spiritual beings in my life. I realized that nothing was final when it came to the passage of time. The soul was eternal, taking on various lessons in each lifetime to develop its level of consciousness. After the experience of one life, another life followed through incarnation, bringing new challenges. The souls interacting within each life were largely the same, each assuming different roles but sharing the same focus on learning.

Chapter Six

New Evidence and Resurrection

In 2021, when I felt I had exhausted whatever I could discover from that past experience, images of a new past life appeared one evening. All I had to do was close my eyes to connect with another reality. I saw myself as a child sitting at a long wooden table. The image began with the wood of the table and then expanded, revealing that I was surrounded by children of various ages also sitting at the table. The room's interior was dark, dimly lit by just a few candles. I was a little girl wearing a white bonnet. I was chewing on a piece of gristle with great pleasure, knowing it was the only piece of meat I would receive that day. In front of me was a metal bowl full of soup, which was more water than anything else, and I had some bread. I felt desperately hungry.

As I lay in my bed in the present, visualizing these images, I also felt the sensation of hunger, which was unfamiliar to me in my present life. While my family and I experienced scarcity in Communist Romania, we never went hungry. Additionally, I didn't like gristle. It was something I had refused to eat during my entire life. In my vision, I was observing myself rather than seeing this experience from the young girl's perspective.

I didn't want to wake up from the semi-hypnotic state I was in— I wanted to feel more. My body felt paralyzed between the two worlds. I was captivated by the visions I was having, and I wanted to stay and explore. However, while I felt my inert body lying on the bed, far away, my mind was telling me that I was in a state between wakefulness and sleep.

Across the table, there was a blond boy with blue eyes smiling at me. He was familiar to me. I knew he wasn't my brother and that he had been raised by my family because he was an orphan. These were details I only knew while being in that reality. Then, glancing at him again for a second, I realized who he was to me. Of course, I recognized the boy in front of me. He was my husband from the recently concluded past life. That boy was Rico in the life where I was Ani.

This was just the beginning of a new journey. Sometimes, during an evening in a meditative state, I would access fragments from multiple lives. When one became uncomfortable and hard to manage, there would be a time jump, and I would enter another body, another century, and take on another role. Sometimes, when I was overwhelmed by the past, I would escape from a past life and enter into my present reality past. I could observe events in the past life as an observer, as if I was watching a 3D movie.

Other times, my consciousness would enter the body of a past life of mine, or I could observe my past life from

Rico's perspective, inside his body. The intensity of the experience was considerably greater when I was in body itself, even though I could quickly depart it if I didn't want to suffer. For instance, I once chose to leave a body out of fear of agony when death was approaching. As I developed more courage, I began to stay in the body and experience it, but even then, before death, my soul would separate from the body, allowing me to observe what was going on from the outside.

The hardest part was witnessing the deaths of loved ones from past lives. Watching them dying or suffering, I felt the emotions in my chest and often woke up crying. It took a few minutes to calm down and understand that those feelings belonged to the past and were not my present emotions. One advantage I had was the ability to exit the cycle of lives I visualized by simply intending to do so. When I decided to quit a specific existence, it usually happened quickly—generally just by waking up.

Afterward, I often stayed awake, trying to understand what was happening and find an explanation for the past. My mind was usually too confused to analyze and offer hypotheses. What resonated within me each time were the emotions I felt, the déjà vu sensations I had since childhood, the things I liked from the past lives I experienced, and the things I hated, all of which I could explain through my visualizations.

The past was pursuing me, and I was allowing it to catch me. In 2022, when visiting Spain, I had some extra time, and I was inspired to enter a torture museum in Toledo. I am not typically attracted to these types of museums; however, I decided to follow my intuition. I was astounded to find a torture device identical to the one described in my first book, *On the Other Side*. Rico had told me about how they used it on him during his mission in Siam (modern-day Thailand). I was so shocked to see it in person, and I kept wondering if he was somehow trying to convince me that we and the memories were real.

That same year, while visiting the Prado Museum in Madrid, I felt physically ill in front of a bust of Nero. I knew his features well and being so close to his face made it seem so lifelike, and I feared for my life. I couldn't get the sound of the whistling arrow out of my mind—the arrow fired by a servant on Nero's orders that struck my husband Alex.

On another occasion, in my dream, I could still hear the screams of tortured prisoners in the catacombs of Rome, where I had spent a few days imprisoned during a past life. I remembered the nightmares I had during my youth, with people being tortured in horrific ways, submerged in baths of molten metal or bricked up alive in walls—images I couldn't explain. Now I knew. The past was ready to reveal itself to me, and I was eager to discover and understand it. There was no greater goal than to know myself and who I was.

I noted everything down. When I wasn't at my laptop, my phone served as my journal. Reaching the moment of death in a past life marked its conclusion for me, and I didn't attempt to uncover more—though at times, new flashes of information would still appear. The information I accessed was usually charged with emotion, either traumatic or very joyful. It seemed I preferred to access those periods of life when the emotions I felt were extreme — whether I was disappointed, hurt, desperate, or, on the contrary, happy. Moments of calm and peace were extremely rare in what I visualized. This didn't mean they didn't exist, but most likely, there was nothing for me to learn from them. They were less accessible to me because they did not generate strong emotional resonance.

Despite undergoing past life regression hypnosis with our former couple's therapist, I was still feeling unfulfilled. I wanted to understand more about the dynamics of these lives and explain the recurring presence of the same person—the shadow, Rico—in the lives I accessed. So, at the end of 2020, just before Christmas, I had a new regression hypnosis session, this time online with someone thousands of kilometers away. It was a recommendation from a friend, and she was the first to briefly mention the existence of Akasha to me.

I tried to understand this concept but only fully grasped it after experiencing the Akashic realm. I have learned the Akashic realm is a dimension where all the life scenarios of a soul—past, present, and potential future—are preserved. Through an altered state of consciousness achieved through meditation or focused thought, a person may access this cosmic database, the Akashic realm, to find information about themselves throughout their past lives. The information about a soul is summarized in a single book, known as the Akashic Records, that exists in the spiritual realm. Directly related to the Akashic Records is the entity, called the "Lord of Records," that represents the guardians of the information in the Book.

The term "Lord of Records" refers to the being who oversees the Akashic Records. The entity is the one who provides authorization regarding how much information is offered, what pieces of information are available, and how that information will be presented to the interested soul from their own Book. The Lord is the one who summarizes the information presented and ensures that only important information relevant to the person's present moment is provided.

The Lord is one of the most mysterious entities I have encountered, and I perceive "him" as an invaluable source of answers regarding any type of questions I might have about metaphysical concepts. Most recently, I have been blessed with the opportunity to communicate directly with the Lord of the Records. Because the Lord of Records is integral to what I describe in this book, I would like to briefly define what I mean by this reference.

Following this regression, I would enter the Akashic realm by myself almost weekly, eager to learn as many details as possible about those lives I hadn't fully accessed. Although hungry for information, the continuous visualizations were exhausting. I felt, acted, and lived like an actor in a new role. The difference was that these roles were real and part of the life I had lived—part of the path my soul had taken. It often happened that I would fall asleep during these visualizations or simply refuse to see more due to the emotional impact on me. It was too much sometimes, yet the information drew me in like a magnet.

I sought a pattern in everything I saw and eventually found one. I repeatedly lived short lives with tragic endings. Despite the different identities and personalities, I retained a core set of characteristics throughout these lives, including my current one. There were traits I could identify in every life without exception that seemed to carry over with me: a desire for independence, defiance of authority, attraction to risk, disregard for rules I didn't believe in, an unrestrained passion for freedom of speech, and the unrestricted ability to explore places where I was inspired to go. What could I learn from these visualizations? Did these traits represent something intrinsic to my soul, like a kind of soul DNA?

It took me quite some time to put all this information into context, and it raised a variety of questions for me. Why was I visualizing them now and for what purpose? What lessons were they trying to teach me about that I needed to do in this life? What was my mission?

My first step in finding these answers was identifying behavioral patterns, fears, and anxieties that I could discover in the memories of these past lives. These were aspects I needed to heal in this life by identifying their past source. I wondered if I could heal by accepting them and creating a connection between the present and the past. In other words, could I heal by acting differently in the future?

The second area I need to examine was the experience itself. Accessing memories from a past that belonged to me in all its complexity indicated that there was much more mystery in this universe. Mystery that I had chosen to ignore in favor of daily worries belonging to our human life and three-dimensional reality. What I needed to do was open my mind and expose myself to as much information as possible, regardless of whether I believed it or not, as it would help me broaden my perspective.

The third area I explored was the circle of people I met. I identified family members, friends, or enemies from my present life playing various roles in my past lives—roles that, while different had a significant impact on my life experience. For example, I discovered that my ex-husband was my friend in Ani's life and that my father from a past life is now Denis, my son. I seemed to be in continuous connection and experimentation with this group of souls across lifetimes. They belonged to me just as much as I belonged to them.

This discovery led me to the conclusion that our experience never truly ends. One could easily frame it as a karmic phenomenon—where a positive or negative action in one life leads to a mirrored experience in another, a kind of compensation. However, I did not believe in this phenomenon of karma and still do not. I do not believe in the existence of an unwritten law that condemns anyone to suffering and forces them to repay or redeem any sins or mistakes. I believe in free will, where each soul experiences certain lessons it wants to learn for its own development.

This soul-learning occurs through our life experiences. Our lives are a form of play for our eternal souls. This play features a storyline similar to my childhood games. In these games, I was in charge, and my soul accepted this role. By agreeing to be incarnated, we choose to be both the director of our own life and the major actor. Only when the role ends do we realize that we are a soul outside the physical shell. It is then that we see if the acting had the success we intended.

In some cases, a poorly played role that has devastating effects on others may lead the soul in question to experience, in a future life, what those other souls once felt. However, it remains the soul's free will to choose whether to undergo the consequences of its actions in order to advance its own level of consciousness.

In the end, the sufferings and joys we experience as we play these roles during our past lives are all part of an immense and continuous game of the universe. It is a game where we try to learn some lessons and test our abilities. Nothing we do or experience is final, and nothing is eternal. The energy we expend is for the purpose of continuous transformation.

These three conclusions have eased my current relationship with my past self. Although the experiences of my previous lives were harsh, I no longer view them with horror, nor do I ask the question, "why me?" They were part of my chosen path. As I look at the traumatic experiences in my past lives, I find it intriguing that I did not suffer from depression. On the contrary, the quality of my current life has significantly improved. I can enjoy my daily routine much more; I am also brighter, more talkative, and more positive. In fact, those close to me tell me I am radiant. In the end, this entire journey of self-discovery has been a blessing, and I have been reborn from the ashes, like the Phoenix of mythology. Rather than being the end, my journey through my reincarnations marked the beginning of a new chapter waiting to unfold.

Chapter Seven

Telepathy and Keeping the Channel Open

I perceived Rico's presence. He wanted to talk to me.

"My body will change. My eyes and hair will be darker. You will not recognize me as I appeared in the past life, but as I am now, in my present incarnation"

Hearing his words in my mind, I burst into uncontrollable tears.

"It means I'm losing you. This is the only way I know you from the past."

He responded, "I will be the same soul, but with a different appearance."

"But why is this happening? What is the need? What is changing between us?"

He calmly replied.

"Nothing... I will appear to you as I am in this life, in my present form. In dreams and other visions, you will see the body I now inhabit. You must become familiar with me as I am today."

I felt his presence disappearing like smoke. *If I lose him too, what will I be left with? Nothing.* My mind kept repeating this to me.

This was the last communication I had in a dream state with Rico, who still was in the body from his last life lived together and who told me that he would appear to me with a different face and body, as he exists in the present. Rico, with the appearance I was used to, began disappearing and was replaced by his present body and personality. Even though he was the man I had loved for so many past lives, he felt unfamiliar to me. I was scared and didn't want anything to change after getting used to him.

I felt comfortable with his presence from our past life, but his message about existing in my present life was causing me to panic and prompting questions in my mind. Why hadn't I met him until now? Would this message of his existence in my present create an obsessive desire within me to find him? I was a wife and a mother in 2020, before my divorce in 2022. How could I ever consider falling in love with him and continue with my life as it was now? I had so many questions about myself. After giving birth, I was feeling unattractive and vulnerable because of my extra weight—and I was confused.

However, I didn't know then what I know now. Even when I accessed my past life memories and saw Rico in them, it was never Rico's presence I was communicating with. The presence associated with Rico's body from our past life seemed detached from that life and appeared independently in my lucid dreams or before falling asleep. I soon learned the presence who told me that the past was over and who encouraged me to relate to the present version of Rico was a being called Xenex.

Xenex is a non-terrestrial entity who had been acting as my guide. He revealed his role and clarified his message step by step, ensuring that I was able to digest the information he was offering as he also calmed my emotions, which were swinging from rage and frustration to peacefulness and curiosity. He started to show me flashes from our last non-terrestrial life together as partners, before we decided to incarnate on Earth nearly 2,200 years ago.

Xenex and I were from different star systems. I was from a planet close to the star Sirius A, while he was from a completely different star system, on a planet called Planet Z. I learned that we met after I attempted to ask for support in a military conflict my planet was facing. Meeting him was a life-changing moment, and we did not part after that. Since my soul needed action and adventure, and my home on Planet Z was a very peaceful place, we decided to take a mission to Earth to study human emotions.

Before the process of my first incarnation on Planet Earth, he split his energy into two. One part of his energy remained in the fifth or sixth dimension to guide me as Xenex and remind me at one point who I was, while the other part incarnated with me as Rico in our terrestrial lives together. Xenex wanted me to understand that his energy was unified: Xenex and Rico are one. The difference between the two presences is that the part of his energy that is Rico has the experience of Earth, while the other does not. However, from time to time, Xenex and

Rico exchange energy to share information and recharge themselves.

I was getting so much information in a short time, it was overwhelming. At first, I was furious about Xenex's presence and my awakening process. I had the impression that I was living in an immense joke and couldn't process everything that was happening to me. Who was I? Was I Ani from my human past life, or was I Aura, the non-terrestrial entity deciding to come to Earth? Who was Rico? Who was Xenex? My mind struggled to process the immensity and implications of everything.

Xenex was gently trying to familiarize me with his dual role. On the one hand, he had acted as a guide from the other dimension, as he explained the reasons for these earthly incarnations and why I was experiencing new spiritual discoveries. On the other hand, he was trying to connect me directly with his energy incarnated in a human body in the present, which was well beyond what he had done previously during his incarnations on Earth.

Xenex made himself known because he didn't want me to remain stuck in past incarnations that had nothing more to offer me. Instead, he wanted me to focus on the present and his presence on Earth, with all that he represented. He wanted me to concentrate on our relationship in the present. He was also trying to make me aware of the existence of multiple realities and he wanted me to understand there were various forms of manifestation that were interdependent.

Xenex, as my guide, was also Rico, with whom I had lived many lives on Earth. Months later, I discovered that I had the same dual role as Xenex, with my energy split in two: one part incarnated on Earth and the other part present in another realm as Aura. I was not surprised. At that point, nothing could surprise me anymore. I was already accustomed to Xenex's presence, and after he had shared so much with me, I trusted him completely. His presence, through his energy footprint, brought me an inner peace and calm that I had never experienced before.

Once Xenex had finished his communication, I eagerly awaited more. I anticipated a manifestation in one way or another, without trying to predict what I might visualize next. After our discussion that night with Rico, along with Xenex's explanations, Rico's appearance from the past had shifted. Though he emitted the same energetic imprint, his physical form was different. It was hard for me to define how.

Despite the same energetic imprint, I could distinguish differences in attitude, character, and his manner of reacting—although I couldn't clearly define physical characteristics. I felt shy in front of this new appearance and wasn't sure how we could communicate. All my connections with Rico's old appearances in the past had broken. The presence of this new man was disconnected from any type of past memory.

But how did everything begin? When the memories of my first past life began to have less impact on my daily life, I started to accept them as they were and placed them in the past and not part of my present life, I began to experience something new and much stranger. The figure of Rico, my constant partner throughout my earthly and non-earthly lives, seemed to detach from the past story itself and appeared quite clearly during lucid dreams and meditation states.

At one point, I realized that I was having telepathic conversations with him. Rico would ask me various questions, to which I would respond. The questions mainly referred to my present life and how the memories of our life together had impacted me. There was a period when I believed it was just self-suggestion, that I was asking myself these questions to compensate for everything I had visualized, even if I perceived these questions as coming from outside of me. I speculated that it could have been a coping mechanism with the past. The explanation would have been simple: I missed this soul with whom I had shared so many incarnations and longed for his continuity in my present life. And indeed, I missed him—and us—deeply.

Despite these questions, the conversations that took place somewhere within my mind gradually took on a more tangible form. There was also a physical appearance of him that I could perceive. This form would fluctuate, replicating one of the known forms from past incarnations. However, one night, the conversation I had with him took a turn. Rico informed me that he would no longer have the appearance from one of our past lives in our future communications, as these appearances belonged to a concluded past. It was time for us to align with the present and what we represent in our current reality. I then realized that what I thought might be self-suggestion was most likely not, as I would not have consciously invented a reason like the one he presented to me.

I had mixed emotions. I did not want his appearances of his past forms to stop. I was comfortable with that past, which I was still learning about. Moreover, the experiences I had visualized about past lives were real to me, and there was no risk of questioning my actual mental health. I did not necessarily want our connection to be translated into a present that felt unclear and ambiguous. Given all this, the information he provided was uncomfortable and unwelcome to me. That said, this was something of a relief, too, as it was also the moment when I became one hundred percent convinced that what I saw and felt was not simply my self-suggestion.

Step by step, in lucid dreams and meditation states, details of clothing and physical characteristics began to appear, such as modern clothing, a body of different stature, and eye color. For example, I could estimate Rico's height as 190-195 cm (6'3" to 6'5") because I only reached the base of his neck when standing next to him. I had also noticed a tattoo on his right hand, but I couldn't clearly define what it represented, even if I knew its size and specific location.

Further, I had clearly seen his arms and the fact that he wore a black electronic watch on his right hand. This intrigued me—I rarely saw people wearing a watch on their right hand and wondered if he was left-handed. Along with that, I had seen a scar on his right thigh and a few on his back, as well as a metal pendant he wore around his neck. Over time, more details appeared as I visualized them, enabling me to create an inventory about Rico's new identity. Though familiar to me through other lives, much of this was foreign in terms of what I had begun to visualize.

I learned from my telepathic communication with Rico and through lucid dreams that he was a few years older than me. I also learned he had been married and divorced, and was American. Along with this, I found out that he was an active officer in the U.S. Air Force, working in communications. I understood that his romantic life was a search for something, and in this search, he hurt a lot of people emotionally. At one point, he was wounded in a military campaign, which led to an operation during which he was clinically dead for a short period of time. That became a point of no return for him. He had completely changed—his character, values, and life goals were different. His military career became his entire life. He got divorced and began searching for the meaning behind the visions he had about past lives. He held strong values about right and wrong and was inflexible about breaking his own values or accepting them being broken by others. Now, I knew he was able to perceive me and understand who I was to him and the impact I had on his past lives. He was in the process of awakening to who I was and how important I had been in his life. I know now that I have been haunting him, just as he had haunted me.

When I perceived him with his new body, dressed in his active-duty uniform, my heart hurt. I had a difficult time accepting his military career and being part of a system I had avoided for a long time. I resisted everything related to the military. For me, the military system was linked to the oppression during Communist times and men who were harsh and aggressive all the time. I also had a short and toxic relationship with a student at the Land Forces Academy who overwhelmed me with his controlling attitude.

Then I remembered that Rico's role in his last past life was also in the active military and intelligence, and because of that, we were involved in many undercover operations that eventually led to me being shot to death and to his suicide years later. Maybe that was why I was afraid even to consider being in touch with a person in the military.

But here he was, listening to all my fears with a smile. Days later, he explained to me that his smile was provoked by my fierce reaction and passionate personality, which he recognized from past lives.

He also knew that our feelings were unchanged by what we did or who we were in any one life. On the other hand, I understood that he was in love with what he was doing and believed in the values of the system, thinking he could make a difference. This belief in fighting for something bigger than ourselves was a value we shared together in many lifetimes, and it was also often the very cause that led to our deaths. Even though I did not always agree with the methods of the military, I admired, respected, and loved him for being so firm in his beliefs.

I couldn't distinguish his face in detail for a long time. If I had needed to create a composite sketch, I wouldn't have been able to draw him. However, I could name details related to eye color, chin shape, lip shape, and hairstyle. I hadn't visualized him as having an ideal physical appearance, and it looked like he was far from what in the past I considered the right type of man for me, yet I knew he was the same man, and his presence meant everything to me. But what was the right type of man for me? Rico was able to confront me in our communication like no other man had. He was firm, decisive, and sometimes inflexible, yet everything he did carried the mark of his desire to protect and love.

I was always able to recognize his energy imprint, and if I was not sure if it was really him, touching him would confirm it. The touch in my visualization was electrical, like receiving a shock. It felt like my dynamic energy was melting. In his presence, I became more fluid and calmer than I typically am.

It took me a while to get used to his new appearance and regain the easy way we communicated. Although our conversations remained regular and consistent, I tried to understand his character in this life, the different aspirations he had, his life history, and his purpose in life. While there were differences from the past, in essence he was the same man from our multiple lives together, with the same values, way of thinking, and acting. He preserved an idealism and energetic imprint that had not changed through many incarnations.

Over time, as our telepathic communications began to unfold, an unexpected dynamic started to occur spontaneously during the day. I could be at work, in the middle of a conversation with someone, when suddenly I would feel strong emotions of longing or love enveloping me. These emotions appeared seemingly out of nowhere while I was absorbed in my work. I was surprised by these inexplicable states where emotions seemed to flood me, and I couldn't identify their origin. The ball of emotions was so strong in my chest that I could feel their pressure, making it difficult to cope with what was happening. At that moment, my concentration would suffer and my breath would shorten as I tried to manage the flow of emotions I was having due to the ones coming from him.

These episodes could last about 30 seconds to a minute, during which I was emotionally consumed with longing and wished I could bite a piece of wood to stop the sensation. Then, as quickly as the emotions and physical reactions appeared, they disappeared as if they had never existed. Although I felt the force of these emotions, I could apparently function normally. Those around me didn't notice any visible change in me, and I did everything possible to mask my feelings. To others, I might have seemed a little distracted and taken deeper breaths than usual at those times.

For a while, I assumed these moments were characteristics of some form of panic attack. However, it was curious that I hadn't developed feelings of fear or a loss of control over myself. None of the feelings of panic, fear, or worry typical of a panic attack were present. When I experienced these sensations, I wasn't afraid that anything could happen to me, nor did I think someone from the outside was deliberately causing me suffering.

On the contrary, the emotions that enveloped me were not negative. Most of the time, they could be described as an intense longing and an unbridled desire for closeness. It felt as if I were waiting for a loved one to walk through the door after a long and difficult separation. I tried hard to find a simple explanation for this state, one that could tie these emotions to my daily life. However, I couldn't explain why these emotional states didn't appear due to listening to a love song or watching a romantic movie. Instead, they appeared when there was nothing to trigger my memory, often when I was focused on a task unrelated to such emotions.

There was no logical explanation. My only conclusion was that these emotions were being transmitted to me by him, as my thoughts then connected directly to his presence. I realized that these emotions didn't belong to me but were somehow projected onto me telepathically. I knew I was connected to him.

In 2023, I was in the middle of a discussion with a potential candidate for a position within the company. While my colleague was talking and asking questions, I felt a presence in the room. I looked at one of the empty chairs around the round table to identify where this sense of energy was coming from. I was able to identify the energetic presence more accurately, positioned on a chair in the room. Although I couldn't see a clear picture as I could with those around me, the energetic presence took shape. I could identify the person's gender, the type of clothing, his posture, and even the expression on his face.

It was unreal what was happening, and I tried to check my state of mind, but it was him—it was Rico. In an extremely short time, we exchanged questions and answers telepathically. The answers were clear, and I perceived them in my mind. We were testing our mood, what we were doing, and where we were at that moment. We realized that both of us were in a meeting. Mine was interesting, but he was bored and playing with a pen between his fingers. After a few moments, the presence disappeared. It was my first strong and clear telepathic experience with him.

These moments repeated themselves and became habitual. It wasn't long before I began to mentally link these spontaneous connections with Rico to times when I was either focused on a single activity, like during an interview, or performing an automatic task like driving or filling out a report. During these moments, my concentration was at its peak, but I also felt a state of maximum relaxation regarding what was happening around me. I assumed this combination of concentration and relaxation heightened the potential for these communications between us.

However, the most difficult moments to adapt to were those when his physical presence did not appear, and there was only the telepathic transmission of his moods, which were harder to decode. I didn't know how to respond to them except to receive them. I also didn't know how many of these telepathic transmissions of his moods and emotions were intentional or if he had the ability to transmit them involuntarily when these states were extremely intense. Certainly, I was a very good receiver of his moods, and these emotions hit me like a lightning rod. They decreased in intensity and calmed down when I intercepted them, especially when I accepted what he sent.

My dilemma was how to handle this new reality. What was I supposed to do with all these states, emotions, and thoughts that I intercepted from him? When I tried to repel them or create a barrier around my chest to avoid feeling them so intensely, it seemed that this form of protection wasn't working. On the contrary, my condition worsened. I became agitated, caught between my attempt to block what I perceived and realizing that I was failing, and the emotions that seemed to float around me.

Over time, I learned that if I allowed myself to feel these emotions and absorb them into my body as if they were my own, they would become more bearable and their impact on me was shorter. I wanted to feel him and know his mood, but sometimes the tumult of emotions was too strong and caught me unprepared. There was no specific topic that would provoke it. I started developing other approaches. I accepted the sensations and emotions he conveyed, and during the time they seemed to be infiltrating my soul, I allowed them to enter and then disappear one by one. They would decrease in intensity and eventually vanish. During this time, I kept reminding myself that these were not my emotions but his, and I took deep breaths to cope with them.

Breathing techniques became one of my best tools. I then decided to respond to these emotions with a flow of love and reassurance, reflecting what I felt he conveyed to me. At that moment, a change occurred. It became much easier for me to deal with such communications in the future. By responding to the flow of emotions, the sometimes-painful intensity of emotions softened and soothed.

Despite the much-needed adjustment I made, it was far easier for me to feel his presence and understand his condition and circumstances than to telepathically experience only his emotions. When he was present in energetic form, I was sure that the communication on his part was telepathic and intentional. Over time, these visualizations grew more sophisticated. I began to see flashes of the activities he was doing, the locations he was in, and sometimes even hearing his conversations with others.

These visualizations were always loaded with a strong emotional imprint. I knew for sure what his mental state was and why he was feeling certain emotions. I could partially perceive his surroundings, such as buildings, parks, houses, and even people. Over time, I learned more about his origin, type of job, hobbies, and even acquaintances. However, I never had a clear picture of everything he perceived at that moment. There were details that weren't clear or that I couldn't perceive at all. I could only hear fragments of his conversations and there were moments when our communication suddenly broke.

My impression was that certain aspects of his life that he didn't want to share were confidential, and he could block them in one form or another. Another possibility was that telepathic transmission didn't always have the same clarity, depending on factors like our concentration and mood. I leaned towards the second explanation because, in later communications, Rico warned me when there were private or confidential issues he preferred I remain unaware of, explaining that it was better for me not to know at that time. If I accepted this, the telepathic communication would cease.

My curiosity grew, and I decided that after so many connections on his behalf, I would test my form of communication with him. I tried several approaches and found that it was enough to focus on his image and make telepathic eye contact with his body to open that channel of communication between us. In these moments when I came into contact with Rico, I felt as if I could transform myself into particles of energy floating around him. At this point, I had the ability to transfer to Rico's location. These particles of energy I sent were absorbed by his body, traversed through him, and emerged into his reality. In either case, these particles would coagulate into a ball of energy. This energy ball, which was me, would place itself near his neck or on his shoulder.

From this position, I could observe what was happening around him. I had the ability to observe in 360 degrees and simultaneously perceive his thoughts, emotions, intentions, and actions. After a while, Rico noticed my presence and usually heard my name whispered telepathically or just checked with a question to see if I was next to him. From the moment we were both aware of each other, we could communicate telepathically without restriction, even while he was interacting with third parties. Later, I preferred to make my presence known to him as soon as I was near him. I could do this with a touch or otherwise by letting him know to avoid surprising him.

These were some of the most controversial experiences I have had during my spiritual awakening journey since 2018. Through my connection with him, I witnessed actions that seemed unclear or highly confidential. Later, I was able to partially verify some of these aspects through public news reports. What intrigued me even more was that my discoveries related to the Ukraine war, which was unfolding just beyond our northern and eastern borders. Because he was in the U.S. Army and involved in NATO affairs, I had some information from our communication that he was working on something related to telecommunications in the Air Force. Due to the war, he was in contact with officials regarding the Ukraine conflict and was stationed in countries close to the Ukrainian border. I worried for Rico—worried because of the war. At the same time, I needed to stay on my path and keep my daily life as it was. My son needed stability, and I did, too.

For me, these communications with Rico were confirmations of our connection. However, without access to more detailed data, I could only rely on the events I could access as an individual. Initially, my curiosity was extreme, trying to find out as much as possible about what he was doing and why. Over time, I learned to be more patient and let him choose to share the information he was comfortable with.

All these communications have only increased the desire for physical closeness between us. Despite all the exchanges of information over the years, we have been unsuccessful in meeting in our current reality, despite several attempts to create an opportunity for both of us to be in the same place and times. Now, after more than four years of wondering why this meeting hasn't happened, despite all the contact we've had and the details we've shared with each other, I believe it's not a coincidence that we haven't met. I feel it's all part of a plan—a plan that wasn't decided by us and that we cannot control, no matter how much we want the same thing.

During one of my regressions, after I learned more about our dual role and non-terrestrial roots, I asked my Higher Self to clarify if we would ever meet again or if it was just our desire to reconnect telepathically, and we would continue this life without each other. The answer came clear: the plan to meet is after the Ukraine war ends. It was then that I understood there is a plan beyond our desires—something greater guiding us.

There were times when what separated us felt like an opaque glass window—something neither of us could see through clearly. On one particular occasion, we both knew when we were in the same location. I could even feel his energy footprint near me, as I expected to run into him around the corner. I had enough physical details to believe I could recognize him anywhere just by paying a little attention. Knowing he was close, but yet not finding him on any of the paths I took was maddening. I felt the pressure of impatience and love, both mine and his, in my chest, along with the hope that this meeting would happen. Then came the frustration of passing one day and then another without any tangible manifestation. I soon felt his energy moving away again, and I knew he had gone farther from me.

However, we never met, and our frustration grew exponentially. We asked ourselves telepathic questions about what was missing to connect the dots for this meeting to take place. Our dependence on these telepathic communications increased, along with the emotional strain we felt as we developed the subtleties of knowing and guessing each other's intentions almost automatically.

We knew each other's lives and began to shape our own lives so that, in the event of a meeting, there would be few barriers between his chaotic life and my life full of responsibilities. Over time, our lives settled into a milder and easier course. I made changes to my location, job, and status, but the most important change we both underwent was that we learned to abandon the control we wanted to impose on our lives and, indirectly, on each other. We learned to focus on the unconditional love for who we are and what we do in this life. The habitual focus on our past relationships and experiences is difficult to undo, but in our telepathic communications, the only constant we concentrate on is who we were beyond our known lives.

I am now certain that our meeting will take place sooner or later, in an unplanned and uncontrolled way. It will happen only when we are both aligned, with ourselves and what we want to do and be. That invisible barrier between us may have existed and it still exists, but we both realize it will disappear the moment we are truly ready for what our meeting means. This reunion will not just be two lovers coming together but will represent much more than that. I believe the consciousness of our souls will align across what was, what is, and what will be, and that all the trauma we have experienced in the past will be fully healed.

Chapter Eight

Entities and Portals

My experience with past lives, telepathic communication with Rico, my connection with Xenex as guide, and learning about the Akashic records were just the beginning of my extraordinary experiences in the non-physical realm. What happened next as I interacted with non-terrestrial beings was totally unexpected and far beyond anything I was prepared for. It was both fantastic and frightening at the same time.

This chapter tells the story of the most challenging and extraordinary set of experiences I have had in my life. Experiences I continue to have to this day. These events have challenged me personally because of the complexity of the information I received and the visualizations I experienced. They raised profound questions about the meaning of what I was going through and how I could translate these experiences. I wondered how my pragmatic mind could accept and integrate them into my reality. Even now, when I read these words, I realize how difficult it is to believe and accept that I have had such experiences—let alone fit them into what I consider normality.

In recent years, I have been living in a whirlwind of sensations, visions, and "aha" moments that I have integrated and accepted. There were two worlds within me. The first world was the one recognizable to all of us, where I had business calls, prepared to become a coach, and behaved as a firm mother and household manager. The other was the world where I wrote about the unbelievable things I was experiencing and seeing. As I read volumes on these topics, I tried to create a bridge between the two worlds. I wanted to understand the differences between them so that I could reconcile the wildly different worlds I lived in. However, until this moment, I was the only thing that they had in common.

In these moments, it is so hard to prove to ourselves that we are still pragmatic, logical, and business-oriented people who operate within normal parameters, and yet there are moments when we can access something extraordinary that has no logical explanation. When this happens, we have no idea how we got to this point or what the expectations are for us to assimilate these experiences into some sort of logical framework. It is this moment when, at some point, we let go of trying to control these experiences and let someone else take the wheel. It is then that we must simply embrace the experiences we do not understand and cannot predict where they will lead. That was where I found myself.

By accessing the Akasha, I had already become familiar with non-terrestrial past lives, but I had not come into contact with any other non-terrestrial presence, except for my guide Xenex. However, this soon began to change. It was as if Xenex had gradually decided to open new doors of knowledge for me. And I was not ready.

My curiosity about the experiences I was going through encouraged me to read about Akasha, past lives, and even UFOs. I decided to keep an open mind and not judge what I read and watched, but to consider them as working hypotheses. I tried to draw parallels between what I was experiencing and the experiences of other people. Nevertheless, on a human and emotional level, I was not ready to engage with anyone beyond the energy of Xenex and Rico.

My contact with non-terrestrial entities began with the appearance of Xenex, and in his presence, I was introduced to two other entities, who were also Pleiadeans. Being in Xenex's presence, I was never taken by surprise or frightened. Additionally, I was able to feel the energy of the beings being introduced to me, which was serene and soothing. The contact was largely telepathic and was no more sophisticated than a simple exchange of information and brief explanations.

Intuitively, I felt that these contacts were preparing me for something more, but I did not ask what it was, nor was I in a hurry to seek explanations, as what I was experiencing was already more than enough. My communications and visions, especially at night, were fluid—in one night, I might access both Rico and Xenex and the Akasha Book. The collection of experiences was still too much, and I felt tired and overwhelmed. To make sense of what I experienced, I tried to find the time to write down what I was seeing. Even though I was curious, I did not want to pursue it beyond interacting with Xenex and Rico.

Xenex understood my slight reluctance to meet new entities and he exposed me to them very gradually. The time spent with them was brief, and the communication would stop spontaneously —usually closed by him or simply fading as I fell asleep. After a while, on a few occasions, two other non-terrestrial species accessed me during visions, providing information about actions I was to take and advising me on how to proceed. While I had some clues as to who they were at the time, it was only later that I learned one was a Grey and the other was probably an Arcturian.

Again, the contact was opened spontaneously, as if I was hearing a voice in my mind, while the voice was accompanied by a mental visualization of the presence. The communication was telepathic. The beings transmitted their energetic imprint during the communication, which I could feel, as they assured me that I was safe. The energy emitted by these two entities was mostly warm, soothing, and gentle. It was like the feeling of being under a blanket, coffee in hand, sitting by the fireplace in my own home.

I soon saw that the most profound and impactful communications with non-terrestrial entities took place in the presence of Rico. Our telepathic communication became deeper day by day, and I was able to connect with him even when he was asleep, visualizing where he was, what he was doing, and staying in his presence for a while. I knew from these communications about his interest in UFOs and non-terrestrial entities. His interest was mostly abstract until one day a profound shift occurred.

One evening, I initiated the connection with Rico and watched him sleeping. This time was different, as I could perceive myself clearly. I appeared as a globe of energy. I seemed to be created from a kind of plasma with blue and white hues, and inside me, lights were flickering like electric lightning.

Most of the time when I spontaneously connected with Rico, the form in which I perceived myself near him was energetic. Sometimes I took the shape of an energetic and luminous globe, and other times, I appeared as a sketched form of a body. Most of the time, I did not analyze the form through which I connected with him, being so happy to be near him energetically.

I acted spontaneously, contrary to my analytical nature, and in this energetic form, I felt free, happy, and comfortable. I did not impose any mental barriers but let myself be guided by intuition, acting based on it. This aspect was different from how Rico reacted, as he was more of an observer who tried to analyze every move he or we made.

This time my energy globe positioned itself on the ceiling of the room, creating the shape of a circle of energy. I perceived it as a portal, as if I created it through my actions. I performed this action automatically, without understanding why I was doing it. It was as if I was creating something familiar but also playing with my own energy. I was experimenting. Soon, I perceived three flashes of light to my right, each having a slightly body-like form and a light-colored energy. They then seemed to materialize from a kind of plasma into three figures, who energetically invited me to accompany them on a journey.

I was shocked, amazed, and confused. Had I, through my energetic play, invited these beings into my life? Who were they? How had they sensed my presence? They did not cause me discomfort; on the contrary, I felt a sense of well-being. But nothing made sense to me. As I felt comfortable in their presence and with a desire to find out more, I decided to follow them.

I accepted their offer, but not before forming a light cord with Rico's chest. I was leaving him behind, and I knew he was not comfortable with me experiencing new things without his presence. Along with that, this cord represented my safety rope, and when I did an astral projection, I was always careful to maintain contact with a vessel. This vessel is always an organic body. In this case it was Rico. I knew that my curiosity and desire to experience something new within my astral connections that I did not fully understand or control, even if seemingly harmless, could also lead to unpleasant surprises. And I did not fully understand the phenomenon.

After a second, I found myself in a room that seemed to belong to a spaceship, which could also have been just a holographic image. But the circular interior of the white hall was familiar to me, as I had been to this place with Rico before.

This was a space where we had been brought together or arrived during our astral journeys from non-physical dimensions. We were familiar with the light-colored, circular interior and the armchair that could transform into a bed. Sometimes, we felt like we were being watched, even though no presence had appeared. We couldn't find a way to access the exterior, no matter how hard we tried. However, it seemed that when we entered this ship, we could do so by simply touching the material it was made from. The material appeared to be organic and flexible, almost liquid, but it could also be dense and translucent at the same time.

This time I perceived a globe of yellow light attached to me, and that's when I realized that I had brought Rico's energy along. He materialized near me in the humanoid form I currently knew, while I retained my form as an energetic globe.

Regardless of the appearance we chose, we could easily recognize each other through our unique energy footprints. I tried to position my energy globe to cover Rico's presence. Ultimately, I felt responsible for him and tried to protect him, not realizing how I had brought him along with me. This gave me the strength to communicate telepathically with whatever might be in that white hall of the ship. I knew we were not alone, and even if we couldn't perceive them, we sensed there were some kind of beings there. This time, though, I saw them and was summoned by them to this space, indicating their desire to communicate with me or with us, and I was growing impatient.

"We are one." I spoke determinedly in English to the beings I knew were in the hall, even if I couldn't perceive them. After I spoke, I perceived them arranged in a semi-circle. Even though I didn't feel threatened, I was trying to provoke a response from them. This was a common way I dealt with these uncertainties. When I visualized entities, there were usually several meetings before they telepathically revealed the purpose for these encounters. While it seemed like they were giving me space to familiarize myself with them, I was impatient. I couldn't get used to just being in their presence, even if I was comfortable with them, without having an action or a response. Even in these spaces, I was the businesswoman who equated time as money, and I couldn't stop myself from rushing to get more information and answers.

"No. You're two. You both are just learning to be one," they responded. Then I felt ejected along with Rico through the portal back to his room.

The fact that they sent us back to the same space where I connected telepathically with Rico, specifically to his room, indicated that the communication was closed. I wonder what would have happened if I hadn't provoked a response? In moments of curiosity or when I felt vulnerable, I reacted spontaneously, directly, uncontrollably, and probably somewhat aggressively. This was most likely the response that led to the closure of the communication.

It was my first experience with a portal. I cannot explain how I was so easily persuaded to walk through that portal with those three light beings. I did not understand how I managed to open that portal by creating the circle of light, and especially why I did it. I did not know if it was curiosity or something else that motivated me to act this way, and I was unsure what those beings I visualized wanted from us. I had no idea who they were or what they represented. Because of their transmitted energy, I felt safe in their presence. I was sure of one thing, though: I did not feel afraid, and I did not falter, although I felt circumspect and slightly suspicious as it happened.

As a result of this experience, the portal appeared spontaneously many times whenever Rico and I found ourselves together in his room, communicating telepathically. The portal often appeared unexpectedly, passing over us no matter where we were in the room, and then it disappeared. There were times when the portal was placed in front of us, waiting for us to decide whether to cross its threshold. It was like a huge door frame touching the ceiling, without a defined door, appearing in tones of dark blue, white, and gray. Nothing could be seen on the other side, as if it were shrouded in fog. If we stepped through the portal, we would not know where we were going until we reached the other side.

I was not familiar with the idea of a portal except on a theoretical level based on what I had read. I assumed it was a gate that, like a wormhole, allowed people to cross spaces and timelines to reach a certain place. By walking through this portal, people could access other worlds, other realities, and possibly other times. This concept had become popular among enthusiasts of non-terrestrial phenomena. The existence of portals supported the hypothesis that non-terrestrial entities could make intergalactic trips to Earth with great ease using this technology. It was assumed that there were natural portals, but there could also be those portals that are created by species with advanced technology and knowledge.

As a result, I started to study more about topics such as non-terrestrial entities, communication methods, and portals. Information in the literature was scarce, so I turned to TV channels that hosted debates and interviews with guests sharing their own experiences with non-terrestrial beings. Each time I came across information or experiences similar to my own, I felt a sense of confirmation that I wasn't the only one.

On a personal level, I also considered that the Book found in the Akasha realm—the one that contained information about me - I believed it formed a portal, allowing me to make my journeys. It was just a feeling and my personal opinion. However, I never visualized this portal in the same way I had seen them in Rico's presence. Instead of appearing as a doorway, it resembled a tunnel that needed to be crossed.

I eventually found myself at a pivotal point in my communications and visions. I didn't understand what was happening, who these beings were, or why I was seeing them in Rico's presence instead of with Xenex, my guide. I felt restless and anxious in my desire to learn more, and I was both suspicious and cautious, as my logical mind was telling me that I was being completely irrational. I sensed that Rico knew more and was much more familiar with these presences.

Thankfully, my curiosity would soon be satisfied. My telepathic communication with Rico was going to place me in other novel situations for both of us. Establishing a telepathic connection, accompanied by the visualization of each other, became a familiar practice, as Rico and I often surprised each other by seeking out one another's presence.

Over time, I had two distinct types of experiences using this portal with Rico, and I realized I could anticipate travelling to one of two destinations.

One of the two destinations placed us in outer space with both of us being a globe of energy and light. The second destination transported us onto a spaceship, the one I mentioned before. Often, when Rico and I were connected telepathically and the portal was present, we saw different non-terrestrial entities. Some of them waited at the entrance of the portal, beckoning us to follow them. Some others appeared close to Rico's bed or in some corner of his room while we were there.

I soon linked the presence of these non-terrestrial entities to the presence of Rico. They seemed to be more connected with him and less with me. I attributed this to the fact that I hadn't had many individual experiences perceiving non-terrestrial species, while I had plenty of them when I was with him. I decided to discuss this with Rico to gain clarity. He vaguely explained that he was in contact with an entity with whom he was having conversations on various topics. He didn't elaborate further, and I knew he was trying to protect both of us by not sharing too much. Now it was time to explore.

"What does the entity you're talking about look like?"

I wanted some physical details and to understand the reason for their discussions. Although I had expressed very little verbally, I tried to convey telepathically all the details that interested me. I wasn't sure if he was in contact with just one entity or multiple entities.

"I don't see it, I just hear and feel it," he answered briefly and clearly.

"But what do you talk about?" I tried to check the type of presence he was feeling.

"We're talking about you, about technology, and about the world in general."

I was puzzled. I asked him, laughing, "But what about me?" I felt him smiling and not willing to continue the conversation about this entity. It was my first attempt to clarify the phenomenon that occurred when I was near him.

I was aware that he couldn't tell me many things because they were confidential, and it was clear he felt that protecting our communication and each other's physical safety was more important. But I liked to challenge him and see to what extent he could provide more details.

My first attempt to clarify the type of entities Rico was in contact with took place in the summer of 2023. This time I arrived alone in the spacecraft with the bright circular hall that was lit everywhere with no discernible source. The walls were almost white with a shiny appearance. In the middle of the hall was the same square armchair, the one I saw that could turn into a bed. I had not discovered how it could transform from one shape to another, as it was a solid object. On this occasion, I did not want to be there.

By accessing my Book through the Akasha realm, I somehow reached this place, but I strongly felt that I was brought here for a purpose. I wasn't afraid because all my previous experiences had been positive and nothing traumatic had happened, but it was contrary to what I wanted to experience at that moment. As a sign of my protest, I began to hit the walls to find an empty space through which I could escape. Even though I was an energetic being, I still behaved as if I had a solid body and didn't know how to act or free myself otherwise.

A telepathic voice spoke to me, "Nothing will happen to you. Stay quiet."

"I want to go out," I said in a firm voice, picturing myself in a shield of white light that was protecting me. Creating a cocoon of light around my body was a technique I discovered in various spiritual books and chose to use whenever I felt the need to protect myself.

At the same time, the interior lit up and blinded me, before I got used to it. I could not identify the source of the light. It seemed to come from everywhere. It was a blue-white light. I noticed, however, that there was a hatch on the ceiling.

"You must respect my free will. I want to go out."

I gave this command because I knew that many species follow the rule of respecting the free will of the beings they contact. The absence of a response to my rather forceful attempts to react made me even more vigilant. It was possible that the entity was giving me space to acclimate to its presence, otherwise anticipating an even stronger reaction from me.

"You people invoke free will, but you do not know what it means. You don't have to be afraid. The human mind is very suspicious, but also extremely curious at the same time. Isn't that why you're here?"

In a sense, the entity was right. I couldn't stop exploring my Akasha Book, whether in the presence of Xenex or Rico. I was constantly pursuing something, though I wasn't sure what. As a result, I was waiting for answers. However, my suspicious nature was beginning to show.

I saw the hatch open like a flower, and I managed to sneak out, where I saw infinity—the cosmos with stars and galaxies. I went in and out several times through the hatch to test my degree of freedom until I came back inside permanently.

"Who are you?" I asked more confidently this time as I was inside the spaceship. I was not fearful, but I was still cautious.

"I'm just a voice now," the being whispered.

"Are you the entity who Rico sees?" I tried to find out more, wondering if there was a connection with him.

"You could say that." the entity answered ambiguously.

It seemed I wouldn't get as much information as I had hoped.

"But why do you want to see both of us? Do you need something from us?"

"Why do you investigate so much? I wanted us to get to know each other," the voice answered softly. These questions and non-specific answers were driving me crazy. Although the emotions didn't manifest as strongly in me as they did in real life, I felt them smoldering deep within my energetic body. I was receiving too much ambiguity from all sides.

"Show yourself," I insisted.

"You will see me in time," came the calm reply.

Gradually, I got the sense that the being was benevolent, and I could lower my guard.

"Are you male or female?"

"I am androgynous."

I felt a headache coming on. My thoughts were unclear, and I remained irritable. When I laid my head on the pillow that night, the headache intensified. I hovered on the edge between sleep and wakefulness, yet the pain persisted—I felt it in that in-between space. I told myself it was because my energetic body was in contact with my physical body.

"Let me help you. Step into that beam of light," I heard the voice whisper.

"I don't trust you. I don't know who you are, or what you are. Besides, the medication I took will help me."

I insisted on keeping a barrier between this being and me. This being that I could just sense in my mind and whose presence I felt around me, but who hadn't manifested physically.

"You humans are interesting. Fear dominates you...but the two of you are starseeds. You need to remember who you are and why you came here."

I understood that this being, whoever it was, knew both of us in detail. Being starseeds meant we had chosen to incarnate on Earth for a specific purpose—a mission we had decided to undertake. However, after so many human past lives, would it still be possible to remember who we were before, or would we see ourselves more as humans, with all the unpleasant traits of a suspicious nature and the survival instincts characteristic of Earthlings?

"I've lived on Earth for so long that I've learned to be cautious like an Earthling."

I was astonished by my own boldness and impertinence in speaking.

"Step into this beam to heal," the voice insisted. But I refused. However, the headache had almost disappeared.

"You're welcome," the voice said.

"What do you want?" I insisted. "Do you just want to talk?"

"We will have time."

Everything faded, and I fell asleep. Once again, I realized that when the entity decided to end the communication, it would shut off like a switch. I could either wake up fully or, conversely, fall asleep almost instantly.

A few days after my first tangible encounter with this entity, I contacted Rico again. His body felt extremely hot while sleeping. As a ball of energy, I was able to view the entire room from above. In front of the bed were tall windows partially covered by heavy curtains with red patterns. I could feel the draft from the open windows reaching me.

Often, when I found him asleep, I would spend time in his presence or wander through the rooms, trying to visualize some of the things he used. This was my way of getting to know him better. There were also many moments when he would wake up, allowing us to communicate telepathically.

This time I looked closely around the room and noticed, at a short distance, an insect-like entity. I immediately knew it was an insectoid non-terrestrial being. I carefully observed its large insect eyes. It had a body similar to a bee's, but its legs were more like those of a spider. At the end of its legs were three claw-like fingers. I did not feel any fear. The entity seemed to be either waiting or standing guard. It telepathically conveyed a sense of calm and tranquility to me.

I was surprised. It felt like every time I approached Rico while he was sleeping, an entity would greet me. Once again, it wasn't clear who it was or what it wanted. Did it have a connection with me, with him, or with both of us? It seemed that our combined presence more frequently triggered this appearance.

I asked telepathically, "What are you doing here?" But it did not want to respond.

I extended my hand, which energetically materialized, and the entity reached out with clawed fingers. They were small hands somehow attached to spider-like legs. Suddenly, another entity appeared beside me. I saw its distinctive blue skin. It was an Arcturian, a non-terrestrial humanoid race distinguished by their bluish skin and hairless scalps.

A moment later, I was on high alert. My energy wrapped around Rico's sleeping presence, and I fell asleep quickly as everything dissolved around me.

Several months later, I discovered that the two entities, the insectoid and the Arcturian, were among the entities whose presence I had felt in the past without seeing them, and they also served as guides. I later saw them in the presence of Xenex and the woman from the Pleiades. To facilitate communication, they even assigned themselves names: the Arcturian named itself Arfa, and the insectoid named itself Arta. Although I could sense the distinct energetic imprint of each entity, they both shared a common characteristic: the calm, peace, and warmth they transmitted. Any protest I felt seemed to dissolve upon contact with their energy, as if I were being enveloped in a vast, comforting embrace.

My original drawing of an insectoid species. This one is similar to a bee.

This experience gave me the courage to explore even further and to show more confidence by at least offering the opportunity to communicate with these beings. My journeys initiated through Akasha or through telepathic connection with Rico continued, and I never knew what I might be exposed to during these journeys.

On one occasion, while accessing the Akasha realm and my Book, I felt myself falling through a tunnel. I was surrounded by flashes that could have been stars or other astral phenomena, which I observed as I passed through the tunnel. The tunnel seemed to be made of plasma, providing me with the possibility to access the cosmos.

For a second, I floated through the ether and suddenly entered the spaceship, the place I had been before. The light inside was extremely bright and white. It blinded me, so I closed my eyes, or what served as eyes in my energy form. It was momentarily dark, and then the walls began to glow. It was a luminous darkness. I touched the walls, and they felt velvety, as if covered in silk, with a cream or white-gray coloring. I was in the craft, in the huge hall, and I could see the armchair that could transform into a bed. Once again, I realized I had known this place for a long time and everything around it was familiar.

I heard a voice that I couldn't identify as male or female, slightly artificial as if produced by some device.

"Do not be afraid."

Then I saw an entity behind me. It had a slightly elongated head with huge insect-like eyes. I couldn't read anything in them; they seemed to be made of thousands of crystals. The lower part of the face was small. I couldn't estimate its height because it stood a few meters away, but compared to my height of 1.70 meters (5'6"), it seemed even taller. It was a Grey, a race characterized by their grey skin tone. They range in height from 1.20 meters to 2 meters (3'11" to 6'6"). Some have large eyes that resemble lenses, and they may have 3, 4, or 5 finger-like digits that extend from a very small palm.

The Grey are composed of several other races that are components of this species. These races may differ in appearance from one another and have various individual characteristics. The Greys could be the subject of a lengthy discussion, but I just want to point out that physical differences can be found, such as the number of fingers present.

"I know this place. This armchair."

I felt excited to be in that place again. This time, it was a feeling of belonging.

"Do not be afraid," the voice repeated.

I was no longer afraid and had begun to get used to these nocturnal visits, regardless of their form. However, the question persisted in my mind.

"What do you want from me?"

"To get to know us," the telepathic response echoed in my head, although I could also hear the voice answering with slightly metallic intonations. This desire to know ourselves, which I knew included Rico, was something I couldn't decode. What did this knowledge mean? It couldn't be physical, as I sensed we were being watched without realizing it. This could explain the presences we sometimes felt around us. Was it knowledge of how we reacted to them? A preparation? For what?

"Do you know Xenex?"

I pressed for a clearer answer. I learned that often, just by mentioning the name of my guide Xenex, I could repel beings that did not align with him in one way or another. Sometimes I would call for his telepathic help, and most of the time he could materialize near me.

"Xenex, yes."

I wasn't sure if this was a positive response or not. "Why me?"

"You are important to us," The entity vaguely responded.

"What do you have to tell me?" I insisted,

"The time will come. Be patient."

I laughed out loud.

"Patience again. I'm tired of this answer."

I was becoming concerned because patience was frequently communicated to me telepathically. And what I lacked was patience. Patience was also a challenging aspect in my daily life, and when placed in these new and unique situations, vague answers completely pushed me out of my comfort zone. But what was I waiting for? Many times, even Xenex, when he didn't consider me ready for answers, used visual metaphors or was simply vague. "You are not ready for more information," he told me at one point.

I moved forward and the entity followed me, but did not come close enough to cause panic. I was just confused, suspicious, and fearful. I turned my gaze and saw another figure, a tall one in front of me, wearing a light gray-white robe like a sarafan. It wasn't Xenex, but it appeared to be someone from his Pleiadian race. I saw that he wore a belt that emitted various lights when touched, had long white hair, and slightly almond-shaped eyes. I recognized him from previous communication.

He telepathically communicated while smiling.

"I have difficulty materializing sometimes in this space."

I was curious about what this space meant, because it was not clear to me what type of dimension I was in. I felt slightly reassured with him by my side.

"Where are the other entities in this room?" I asked silently in a telepathic mode.

"We are here, along with other races." The answer was whispered.

Then I understood that from the beginning, there was a welcoming group that joined the other entities present, who, for various reasons, did not want to be seen.

I then saw what appeared to be a woman with an almost triangular head, dark blue skin, and a small face. She was short in stature, about 1 meter tall (39"). The entity was Erfa; I recognized her from previous communication.

Then Rico appeared by my side, curious about how I had arrived here. His question confirmed my idea that he visited these places more often and was more familiar with the various presences of other species—or perhaps he was simply more relaxed around them.

"I came to see what they want," I responded.

I observed them offering him something to drink, a colorless substance, which he accepted gladly.

With a warm smile, he reassured me.

"This isn't the first time I've been here. I've met them before."

"And what are you drinking? What is it?" I sought clarification.

"It's a purification substance."

As well as his words, he sent me telepathic images that demonstrated how the colorless substance purified the energetic body in a certain way. The communication stopped. Somewhere along the way, the communication was either stopped by those entities, or I simply fell asleep. Most of the time, it was difficult for me to identify exactly what happened.

Nevertheless, these enigmatic journeys didn't stop. Intuitively, I felt that their importance was growing, and both their openness and mine increased with each interaction. There were more moments when I came into direct contact with them without being in Rico's presence, and I no longer felt the need for an intermediary in this communication, such as Xenex.

At the same time, these communications could occur spontaneously. It was no longer necessary to connect with Rico through telepathy or go through the Akashic space. Messages and images appeared as if they were engraved in my mind. They could happen at any time, including during the day, especially when I was doing routine or repetitive tasks. Usually, they were short and meant to convey brief messages.

At first, I was amazed and delighted, but other times I was annoyed that this unseen world was crossing a boundary I had clearly created between my daily life and my astral existence. I constantly checked my mood and mental sharpness as a way to control myself. I was too tired to analyze what was happening to me. It was hard for me to talk about them and even to hear myself speak, because my experiences seemed so incredible that they sounded false—even to me. But I was about to find out more.

On a summer afternoon, I fell into a kind of trance as soon as I laid my head on the pillow. I felt like I was lying on Rico's chest, but the hand caressing my shoulder was not his. It felt strange. The hand was something grey. Lifting my head, I saw a Grey next to me, tall with a bulbous head, though perhaps not a Grey in the true sense of the word, but similar looking. It gestured for me to follow, and the voice communicating telepathically was womanly Seeing my hesitation, it beckoned with its hand. Its body was bony and thin, with a bulbous head, but its gaze seemed human. Its eyes were smaller and more expressive than what I had seen previously from Greys. One of its fingers touched the air in front of it, creating concentric circles as if it had touched water or a fluid surface. On the surface, what looked like green laser writing appeared. It seemed to be cuneiform script: a vertical line with a diagonal line at the top, a dot, then a diagonal line with two dots on either side.

My original drawing of the writing I saw.

I was in shock. It seemed to me that I was facing a monumental discovery and had the honor of being the first. But of course, what I saw did not translate into understanding. I watched in amazement, jumping from one line to another, trying to remember them. I approached and finally touched the first symbol. It opened like a mirror, revealing a new surface like water. I could see on the surface a star with two planets orbiting it. Soon, I perceived myself entering the image and I was on the spaceship again, surrounded by non-terrestrial entities. The writing itself and the actions I had taken seemed to open a portal that allowed me to reach the same familiar spaceship.

I noticed that my left, diagonally, was the same Grey entity I had seen before. Next to me on the left was a humanoid entity very similar to those of us in the human race on Earth, with red hair. I knew it was non-terrestrial.

"I don't think she's ready," the man with red hair said clearly.

In front of me was the Pleiadian woman who I knew before. She approached me. Pleiadians are a humanoid race that closely resemble Nordic humans in their appearances. They are very tall, ranging from 1.80 (5'11") to 2.50 (8'2") meters, with white skin, white or blond hair, and athletic bodies.

She was stunningly beautiful.

"Welcome," she spoke to me in English. "It is time for you to know."

English was spoken rarely, and it seemed like they were trying to pronounce it correctly and somewhat forcefully to ensure it was understood, or it was simply difficult for them to pronounce the sounds.

I fell into numbness, almost falling asleep. But the Pleiadian woman appeared again, and my awareness was focused. She then spoke to me.

"Volvo alemida sa."

I was amazed. She repeated these words to me several times to help me remember and transcribe them after, but I had no idea what they meant. The sounds felt strange in my mouth and somehow carried a weight that I could only sense.

Then she said. "Ti kara."

Again, I had no idea what they meant or why she was telling me, but I could see that she gave importance to these words. She spoke in a warm tone and with great care, as if offering me a precious gift. I felt that she expected me to recognize their meaning, but I couldn't.

Then I saw Xenex materializing next to her. The woman turned to him and spoke to him clearly.

"Ta kiki ta." She repeated insistently, but Xenex did not react.

Eventually, as if by command, I woke up from my hypnotic state. I had fallen asleep.

Following this communication, I started an online search. I was convinced that I could find a translation or meaning in one of the ancient languages for what she told me. Thus, I found out that "Ti kara" means 'durable' in Hindi. However, for the phrase "Volvo alemida sa," I couldn't find something relatable. For "Ta ki ta," I found a meaning in Nepali, which means pressure; urgency; reminder.

One thing was clear to me: the Pleiadian woman told me those words and repeated them so I would remember something. She insisted on being present with Xenex to help convince him of something I didn't understand and that Xenex seemed reluctant to implement.

But with each new communication, the fog I felt during these communications seemed to dissipate, and I gained more clarity. What exactly was expected of me?

The next encounter found me in a state between sleep and wakefulness. I saw images after closing my eyes, surrounded by a foggy environment where details were blurred. I waited because there was something that always appeared in front of me. This time an unknown Pleiadian man appeared— he had wavy blond hair, blue eyes, slightly loose pants, and a kind of tunic with a belt around the middle. He then gently spoke.

"Are you ready?"

Curiously, he did not wait for an answer, but I sensed an energy from him that comforted me.

"Who are you?" I asked.

"You will find out later," he answered with understanding.

He was such a beautiful being that I thought about how humanity historically has defined angels and archangels; his presence conjured up similar visions. He noticed telepathically my thoughts and smiled.

"What should I be prepared for?" I asked him verbally.

"You will do a kind of channeling," he transmitted telepathically.

"So, will an entity attempt to express itself through me?"

I was not comfortable with that thought. I knew what channeling meant from what I had read, and the idea of allowing any type of entity, even one I was familiar with, to flood my consciousness seemed extremely uncomfortable. I couldn't accept myself in this role. I think she sensed my reluctance.

"Not like that. You will receive information and knowledge. First for you, then some of it you can write or talk about." This time he expressed himself verbally. I sensed he was trying to convince me.

"So, it is not channeling," I insisted.

"It might be another word to describe it." He responded softly.

It seemed we were both searching for it, but I couldn't pronounce it.

"In short, I encourage you to write and publish."

He was direct, warm and firm at the same time. I was amazed at the certainty with which he conveyed these ideas.

"But I don't know how. It seems hard to achieve much impact as an indie author."

At that moment, I wondered if this direct message was due to my doubts about whether to publish my second book, which included discussions I had with Xenex, my guide, on various topics, as well as with other entities. I wasn't sure if I wanted to expose myself to the public with such personal, mysterious messages that could be considered completely fantastical. Could this message from him be related to that?

"You will be guided. You both have a lot of work to do."

I noticed how he tried to assure me that everything was guided in one way or another

A purple entity, Erfa, and an EBEN came in front of me shortly. EBEN is a subgroup of the Grey race. Their characteristics are similar to those I described for the Grey species. However, I felt comfortable in the presence of EBENs, which was not the case with other Greys. The EBEN addressed the Pleiadian man telepathically; however, I was able to intercept their communication.

"So you convinced her. Congratulations."

Erfa seemed happy, expressing its joy through a kind of dance.

"Are you able to dance?" I asked.

"Of course. Why wouldn't we? It is not just a human characteristic. And when you are just an entity of energy you can launch yourself on other frequency waves and combining them you can create astral dances."

I was struggling to understand the parallel he was making between the somewhat grotesque and comical movements he was making and the cosmic dance of an energetic entity. But my thoughts were more inclined towards a cosmic dance. Neither of us had any idea if what I understood was indeed the meaning of what he wanted to communicate to me. However, because of the emotion I felt from Erfa and his desire for emotional closeness to me, I felt that I intercepted it correctly

It was at this point the communication stopped, and I awakened back in my third-dimensional reality.

What I have described so far were comfortable encounters during which I relaxed and was able to later enjoy what I was transmitting or what was being transmitted to me. However, there were also moments when the survival instinct took control of the communication, moments when I was scared and felt alone and completely helpless for a while. In particular, I had such an encounter and communication with a reptilian being, most likely a Draco, a sub-species of reptilian, who are warrior-like with a strong tail and body. They also project a more negative energy imprint, whether that's intentional or not.

My communication with this entity happened two or three times until it was eventually stopped by Xenex. Each time, I encountered it in the presence of Rico while I was connecting telepathically with him, and each time Rico was in a deep sleep. I have developed a certain method for making this connection with him, and often these steps are unexpected. They can even surprise me, as I have been making this connection with him for many months. This time, I will describe it in detail.

I connected telepathically with Rico's body and energetically entered inside him. I visualized his interior as silver-colored with a beam of fluorescent blue light that produced a buzzing sound. My form disintegrated, and I transformed into lilac-colored dust. The beam of light also transformed into a kind of plasma that integrated my particles within it. Finally, after traversing his body, I exited as particles through the skin of Rico's shoulders and face. I was now in the place where he was, appearing as simple dust particles floating in the air.

It was dark, but I saw a luminous line, a streak, coming from the closed blinds. Rico was sleeping deeply. When I turned my gaze from the edge of his bed to the wall, I saw a silhouette. It looked like a Grey. It was about 1.40 (4'7") - 1.50 (4'11") meters tall, with black eyes that seemed to reflect light and appeared more like mirrors. I saw the Grey extending a small hand with five fingers towards me. I did not respond with any gesture, but telepathically I enveloped myself in a cocoon of light and did the same for Rico's body. This method of creating a shield, which I often used, brought me comfort and peace, and I perceived it as my protection.

I was on the defensive. The desire to be touched raised my suspicions, and moreover, my encounters with the Greys were always problematic. I could not feel their energetic imprint in any way; they seemed slippery to me, and I had received some suspicious proposals from them. Unlike the EBEN, whom I could feel energetically, with this small Grey form, I did not know what to expect.

Then I turned my gaze to the foot of the bed where Rico was sleeping, and there was a reptilian being. Reptilians are a race that resemble reptiles as we know them on Earth.

However, they have human-like features, including two legs, two arms, and a head. It is common to see them with snake-like skin and a tail. They are quite large and tall, and I experienced a sense of aggressiveness from them.

This one was at least two (6'6") meters tall, with muscular legs but bizarre joints, a combination of human and reptilian, allowing it to move horizontally and vertically with the same ease. The arms and chest had a human-like appearance, and the skin was scaly and green. The head had two large yellow eyes with retractable pupils. The mouth resembled that of a lizard. The body had a lizard-like tail and a kind of crest on the back. I sensed from the nature of its energy that he was a male specimen and was trying, to a small extent, to leave his energetic imprint. Even so, he provoked fear in me. I stared at it for a long time, and we measured each other for a while.

I telepathically conveyed to him that both Rico and I were protected. I felt a subtle energetic wave coming from him, which I did not perceive as positive and benevolent, but he only allowed me to feel it in a reduced form. He retracted his pupils and, although his face showed no expression, he seemed to grin as he responded,

"That's right. Rico is protected. But you are not. You are part of the same energy as far as I know. Only his part is protected now. And you are not."

He telepathically transmitted an image of my energetic body connected to my physical vessel by a silver cord, showing that I was exposed and vulnerable. I had the feeling that he was cynical and was openly showing me that he was in control of what was happening at that moment. And I knew that was the case. However, I could be extremely cautious. Perhaps I could at most distract him, but then I remembered that my thoughts could be intercepted, and I didn't know how to block them based on the experiences I had had so far.

"Why have you come?" I asked firmly.

"To see you and to know you," He replied telepathically looking closely with his yellow eyes.

"For what purpose?" I insisted.

"I have heard about you two and I wanted to see what you represent. I wanted to introduce myself," he responded, his telepathic voice occasionally accompanied by a strange, audible growl. I was trying my hardest not to let fear take hold of me because I sensed that he would have been satisfied with the effect it would have had on me.

"What do you want?" I asked cautiously.

"For now, nothing."

I sensed that he did not want to cause me too much fear. But why was he still behaving cautiously? In the end, I probably wasn't as alone in this space as I had thought.

"What do you want?" He did not respond, and I noticed that a Pleiadian man appeared nearby, tall with white hair. I did not perceive him clearly. He first positioned himself behind the reptilian and then moved to appear from the side. The Pleiadian man told him: "Ashiii kala." He repeated the phrase for a long time, hoping to provoke or remind the reptilian of something. The reptilian disappeared after.

From previous experience, I knew that if Xenex did not appear in these cases, most likely someone from his race would show up, as in this case. Although I did not understand what was communicated in a hissing tone, it convinced the reptilian to disappear as quickly as possible. As before, I verified the words spoken. Again, I managed to identify a possible meaning in Hindi: 'moon.' But what could such a meaning conceal?

My original drawing of the Reptilian species I saw. Possible Draco.

These are some fragments of the encounters with various non-terrestrial species that I had over the course of two years. I could roughly identify some of these non-terrestrial beings based on the materials I read before. That's why it seemed important to present the sketches I made after seeing them, which I kept intact to avoid altering the image in any way.

There have been numerous appearances of non-terrestrial entities in my visualizations and many moments when I could not identify the reason for their appearance or their desire to communicate. In some cases, it was probably curiosity towards me or Rico; in other cases, it was just an act of observation or perhaps a warning, or even an attempt to urge me to take certain actions. There were a few moments when the entities I saw did not inspire confidence, and I felt afraid, as was the case with the reptilian species. The type of vibration he transmitted caused me chills, prompting me to be cautious every time. Although I'm not entirely sure their intention was malicious, I interpreted his energy that way. As I have only perceived a single reptilian specimen, at least from my knowledge, it is difficult for me to conclude that any reptilian specimen provokes the same energetic imprint through its presence. I simply do not know.

There were other non-terrestrial entities in whose presence I felt comfortable from the very first contact. This was the case with Erfa, probably an Arcturian, or Arta, the insectoid. Whenever I encountered a new entity, I tried to identify the vibrational waves as quickly as possible and determine if they aligned with a feeling of comfort and well-being.

It is difficult for me to identify the dimension where these encounters took place. It might be in the fifth or sixth dimension in which all the entities are more of an energetic projection and not organically based, even though they might leave the impression of being organic.

I perceived meetings taking place on a spaceship that had either a spherical or disc-like form. There were moments when the background where I was appeared empty, and no details could be observed, making it difficult for me to understand the place. My state of consciousness during these moments hovered somewhere between wakefulness and sleep. After a communication ended, I would either fall asleep without realizing it, meaning I didn't know if the communication continued or ended and I subsequently fell asleep, or I would suddenly startle and wake up completely. I perceived myself in their presence as energy, although I could retain the characteristics of my human body, more like a physical imprint. However, there were moments when my presence manifested more as an energetic ball.

These encounters did not only occur in Rico's presence. I was accessed even in his absence. However, I always had the feeling that he was more familiar with these entities than I was and could guess their intentions much more easily, and by extension, they were also interested in me. But there were also entities that came specifically for me, to guide and protect me. The portal I perceived in Rico's presence was certainly an open channel for these communications.

Even so, I perceived the existence of the portal in other circumstances as well. The experience of the second destination through the portal occurred at the beginning of 2023. I followed the same steps and connected to Rico telepathically. I was shaped like an energy globe and attached myself to his chest. The room was dark, but suddenly, a column of yellow energy formed in front of the bed. My energy globe began to revolve around the column of light, drawn to it like a magnet. I saw an arc of white-gold energy form, with a silver-blue interior. I approached and was tempted to walk through this arch. But Rico woke up, sensing my intention, and I saw him holding me by his side, creating a white energy cord between our hearts. I insisted on moving through this portal.

At that time, I was the one initiating these explorations and he was more cautious. Eventually, we stepped into our humanoid forms, composed solely of energy, through the formed tunnel. As we advanced, we gradually lost our humanoid shapes and transformed into energy globes, gaining speed and becoming two energetic spheres of different colors. I didn't realize when we changed shapes. An energetic exchange occurred between the two globes, appearing as lightning discharges followed by sparks, and eventually, like magnets, as we became a single globe. We were together in this nest yet still separate in our energy. The characteristic colors of our energies only mixed slightly.

The end of the tunnel looked like a black mouth with white edges, and at that moment, we were thrown out into the cosmos at high speed. At that moment, our energies became complementary—mine manifested a desire for action and exploration without considering consequences, while Rico's energy felt heavier, more static, and contemplative. I couldn't determine the direction of our movement: whether it was up-down or right-left. We stopped moving and somehow remained suspended in space. Around us appeared energy globes similar to ours, which I identified as souls. They transmitted white light flashes to us at a certain frequency, which I perceived more as a form of healing. Then they changed the frequency level, and I felt our combined globe being impacted. As a result, we were sucked back into the tunnel and thrown onto the bed in our humanoid forms.

These experiences remain among the most beautiful feelings and perceptions I have ever had during these visions. The feeling of perfection, bliss, and beauty is hard to convey through language. I felt complete, needing nothing and asking nothing from anyone. I felt whole.

In a future chapter, "Being a Ball of Light," I will present more details about how the transformation takes place from a humanoid form into an energetic and light globe, the abilities we possess as a result of this form of manifestation, the way of manifestation, and the restrictions. For me, this form of manifestation is preferred when I have these astral projections. The freedom and ecstasy felt cannot be equated with any other human emotion as I know it.

The most problematic aspect, however, remains the will to return to the vessel I am bound to as a soul. Intuitively, I perceived that after a longer period spent on an astral journey, there is a desire to stay as long as possible in this realm, which may be counterproductive to the existing body and the pre-plan of that soul, as it diminishes the desire to return.

In conclusion, the telepathic act with Rico, accessing the portal, and communicating with various non-terrestrial entities, whether energetic or not, was not just an act of will on my part but one of mutuality. There were moments when I could easily access Rico telepathically, or he could access me, in a natural, spontaneous, and effortless way, just like any action we perform during the day. For a while, I considered it as given, a gift that, once received, could not be taken away, and thus nothing could disturb the manner and timing of our desired contact. However, I later learned that there are also moments when, no matter how much I wanted to access anything, it was not possible. It was as if all my experience with other realms did not exist, and any contact was denied. I felt completely disconnected from any method I had tested over time and with which I had had success.

I have experienced these interruptions in contact several times recently, alternating between periods of intense communication—accompanied by deep fatigue, exhilaration, and the satisfaction of my curiosity—and periods of overwhelming pressure during the day as I tried to cope with human problems while also finding time to record what I had received. On the other hand, there were moments of relaxation and unwinding in the absence of contact and recovery of daily reality, but also frustration because communication was denied.

Again, I found myself at the boundary of the two worlds, wishing to exist in both, but for them to be so well delineated that I could only choose when to exist in one or the other. But the two began to merge, raising questions about how I would be able to cope in the future. My refuge was trying to translate what I had seen into a form of hypothesis, partially having a logical explanation.

In my attempt to analyze the possible sources of these fluctuations in my communication with non-terrestrials or even Rico, I managed to conclude there were two of them.

One possible source was myself, with my mood, my fatigue, and my concerns. My daily life, the people I came into contact with, and even the relationships I still maintained with toxic people affected my energetic field and personal space. Even the fact that I was introducing these people into my personal space and my house could cause fluctuations in my visions. Because they came with a variety of vibrations and energies and could cause as a blur during my visualization, they could cause problems for me in creating connections. So, I decided to be more attentive to those I interact with and also how much I bring them into my personal space. I have become more selective with my time spent with people who bring only a vibrational level that charges me.

A second possible source for the fluctuation was certainly the receiver, in this case, Rico or any other being from another dimension. The contact was supposed to be mutual and guided by free will. Without the consent and intention to connect from the entity or Rico, nothing happened. It was an act of my will and that of the other side, and because of this, the channel of communication was closing.

These experiences with meeting and communicating with various non-terrestrial entities and accessing portals, have been some of the most challenging and rewarding experiences I have had. There were moments when I wished this type of communication would stop. I didn't understand it; it pulled me out of my comfort zone and made it hard to talk about. These experiences were almost impossible to accept and difficult to integrate into my belief system.

Despite all this, what I learned through these experiences is that there is something beyond us humans and our world on Earth.

I learned that there are non-terrestrial beings who, by their mere presence near me, can influence my mood and make me feel comfortable, happy, and satisfied with my condition, or, on the contrary, can provoke fear and panic.

I learned to decipher their energetic imprint and to telepathically transmit what I feel or think through words or through images and concepts, and I discovered that this act is of rare intimacy and beauty.

I learned to have the courage to accept the invitation to access portals and to reach spaceships where I let myself be surprised by the reason I was brought to that place.

I learned to explore where I had gone and, above all, not to be afraid. I learned to be brave and to express any fear I might have because, in the presence of many of the non-terrestrial entities I met, I found understanding and comfort.

What I also learned is that many of these species may have difficulty understanding the diversity of human emotions, especially the negative ones. This helped them see how we allow ourselves to be influenced by them without using our logical side.

I also learned that it is sometimes difficult for them to convey a message or explanation in the way we humans are used to. They tend to use a metaphorical language that they enrich with images and concepts. These communications, when translated into language, may seem sophisticated, unclear, and sometimes confusing. However, all these communications are beautiful. The absence of a common language between both parties makes simple, elegant communication through the energetic imprint possible. This method can convey not only emotions but also information and a strong sense of well-being.

A profound realization I took away from my experiences is the knowledge of other worlds and entities who can have a system of thinking, feeling, and organization so different from what we're used to that it can only be known through maximum openness on our part. It has been my experience that the vast majority of entities, if contact is rejected or if communication is refused, will not insist on communicating and will respect the human's refusal by withdrawing from the situation. For those who haven't had contact experiences in the past, the simple possibility of exploring the existence of other worlds and knowing the existence of other entities can broaden our perspectives.

Another concept that I have become far more comfortable with is that of telepathy. Each of us has experienced moments when, just by thinking about a person, they contacted us shortly after. For all of us, there have been many other times when what we were thinking manifested in a tangible form. Our thoughts take shape outside the language we use, and the power of telepathic communication—especially when accompanied by strong intention—is much more powerful than language alone because what we transmit reaches the receiver, even if we do not desire this. It's as if our thoughts are radio waves moving through the air towards a receiver, and they produce effects regardless of whether we realize it or accept it. The intensity of our intention can manifest what we focus upon, even if we are not aware of our abilities.

The final thing I discovered from these experiences is the enormous complexity of human emotions. Many times, in communication with non-terrestrial entities, I felt that they failed to understand our survival instinct and our tendency to go into defense mode when confronted with uncertainty. Even if they might understand our reaction logically and scientifically, they fail to grasp the intensity of our negative emotions and how these emotions can divert us from our intentions and impact how we react. The same goes for positive emotions. The positive emotions I felt coming from them, whether it was love, compassion, or empathy, were presented to me in a very calm and balanced manner. From this perspective, we were certainly interesting to them because of the intensity of our emotion—and my tendency to act impulsively.

These extraordinary experiences were so powerful that they affected all areas of my life. As a result, I struggled with doubts and fears whenever I tried to talk about them.

Chapter Nine

Doubts

"When will we get there, mom?" my little boy asked in a faint voice.

I looked at Denis lovingly. Intuitively, I knew he had been one of the catalysts for the changes in my life. For someone so young, the immense energy and wisdom he displayed sometimes shocked me. At five and a half years old, he knew his mom was a writer. He was the first to give his opinion on the cover and sometimes asked me what was new in my writer's life. At one point, his father had asked him what his mom did for a living.

He answered confidently, "Mom writes."

I had also started drawing again after years of not touching a sheet of paper. And Denis was delighted. I wanted to express as much as possible of what I saw in my lucid dreams and meditation states. I needed to draw the strange spaces I found myself in and the figures of entities I perceived. All these visualizations had been the starting point for my second book. I had an enormous need to express myself—a need that was so obsessive it often scared me. I couldn't explain why this urge had been so deeply buried within me and how suddenly everything surfaced. Although Denis demanded so much of my free time, he was the one who expressed the most curiosity and encouraged me to continue.

It was July 2024. It was a scorching day, and I was dragging myself along with him towards a children's workshop. We tried to keep cool by skirting under the shade of the few trees, but we were exhausted. I felt my energy draining with every step. In fact, my lack of energy had been persisting for several days. I was in the middle of preparing for the launch of my second book. I had doubts about what I was doing. I wasn't sure I wanted to continue this journey.

After receiving three rejections from three foreign publishers for my first book *On the Other Side*, I decided to self-publish my two books. Becoming a self-published author is very difficult, and I made innumerable mistakes in my solo launch. My mistakes cost me financially as well as all the time lost from going in various unproductive directions without having a consistent marketing strategy.

The good news is that I had learned a lot and gained experience about the entire self-publishing process. I now knew that the book itself mattered less than I thought when it came to sales. What mattered more was choosing the most appropriate target audience for my book, how I positioned myself in the market, and choosing the optimum timing for my book launch. With my first book, I had chosen everything wrong from the beginning. But I felt that I was publishing it more for him—for Rico— and to remind myself who we were together and what connects us in the present.

Now, my mind was far away. I was analyzing how I could successfully start over with a second book, *Conver-*

sation with Xenex, which would be a continuation of my awakening journey and much more intimate than the first book. It represented a new step in revealing myself, with all the doubts, fears, and inner struggles I had. It would also describe the beauty of being in contact with another realm—the astral one. Along with that, *Conversation* was a book I believed in with every fiber of my being.

Because it meant so much, I didn't want to repeat the marketing mistakes I had made with my first book. It was important to me that the message be conveyed correctly to the reader, even if it sometimes might sound unreal. Most importantly, this was a book that non-terrestrial entities and the Lord of Records had instructed me to write and publish.

When my desire to continue with publishing began to fade, the message received from them was brief and categorical. I was told the information received was not just for me; it was meant to be conveyed to those who wanted to hear it. I learned if I didn't follow through with writing and publishing this book, I would either do it later, or another person would take it over from me. I understood the book already had a life of its own. It did not belong to me.

This reminded me of my adolescence when I helped Ina, my mother, with the choreography of certain dances. I enjoyed it and created complex choreographies for various ballet shows with boundless pleasure. However, once the dance was finished, I saw that it no longer belonged to me. It became independent and had a life of its own. I was like a mother who parted with her child, accepting it with its beauty and flaws.

It was then I knew *Conversation with Xenex* would be controversial and expose me to possibly unpleasant reactions.

I presented my books as non-fiction, under the category of spirituality. However, in both the first book and the second book, what I wrote about did not fit comfortably into any area of spirituality.

In the first book, I talked about my initial experience with past life memories and mostly told my story as I visualized it. I knew there would be readers who would contest the authenticity of the memories and consider it more of a tragic story and nothing more. For me, it represented past wounds I was expressing in writing, trying to heal a past that was the beginning of everything. The second book was very different. This time, I was entering a zone of radical new age thought. The experiences I recounted could seem incredible due to the exotic nature of the subject.

As I searched for the right category for my books, I saw they didn't belong in the self-help zone, nor were they books that could be supported by scientific evidence. Still, I felt that both books clearly presented my own spiritual experiences and the turmoil I had gone through on my journey—a journey that changed my life's path, values, and perceptions. Those experiences had shaped my decisions, and I continued to exist in my day-to-day life through the lens of what I had gone through.

Even after I had finished the two books, I continued to face two burning questions. Had all this effort been worth it? Was it worth dedicating myself to writing when there were so many other things in my life that needed attention? My little boy? My job and business life? What about my budget, house, expenses, vacations, etc.? And then there was my overwhelming urge to write. Where did this need come from?

I didn't feel that I had to prove anything to anyone. Yet, there was still this urge to write. I had promised myself that with the second book, I would close this chapter of my life. I would stop writing. I had promised myself that I would have more time for myself and would dedicate time and finances to investing in my family, maybe also to traveling. Moreover, why not? I would remember that I exist as a woman, too. Maybe I could give myself the chance to explore this direction, even if Rico was not physically present in this NOW with me.

But where did the hesitation come from? Early on, I decided to write under a pseudonym: Adria Sanders. Both the first and last names belonged to me to some extent. As for the specifics of the pseudonym, I had the name Adria in a life thousands of years ago during Nero's reign in ancient Rome, and Sanders belonged to my partner in one of my past lives. But why didn't I have the courage to own everything I wrote under my real name? Fear of judgment?

I believe part of my hesitation was because my real name partly belonged to my father, with whom I had little connection, and another part was associated with my ex-husband. I didn't feel either name represented me on this new path. The second reason for my hesitation was my reluctance to let my company know about this part of my life. By its very nature, my writing could impact my credibility in the world where I operate as a career woman.

I was involved in business, where logic, pragmatism, and balance were required. How could my spiritual visions align with what I lived day-to-day in the company? Astral projection? Conversations with non-terrestrial entities? Or even simple memories of past terrestrial or non-terrestrial lives? No, I didn't want to enter into such discussions with my colleagues where I had to explain my association with these subjects. It continues to be a private area.

Returning to that day in July 2024, my son and I headed to a children's workshop. When we arrived, it was being held in a house with a shady garden. At first, my little boy seemed interested. He tried to make new friends on the small football field. I sat down on a tree stump that served as a chair. I glanced at my author page on the Amazon site and saw the sales statistics for my first book. I frowned. Even the simple act of sitting and checking stats tired me today. But why was I doing it? Why did I continue? My logical side echoed my grandmother's voice in my mind.

"You've already invested in the second book. It's almost ready for publication, and you want to stop? That's not like you. What you've started, you must finish, then you can stop."

My family's childhood encouragement still had strong roots in me. However, over the past few days, out of nowhere, I started having ideas for a third book. I stopped what I was doing and began to write spontaneously. I wrote with pleasure and without thinking too much. Was it just my desire that prompted my writing, or was there external guidance? Was it the same guidance I had when I wrote *Conversation with Xenex*? I sighed deeply. What I knew for sure was that I was being driven by my own desires. The astral guidance I received was uplifting during the creation process, but it didn't help me through the practical realities of publishing a book, marketing my book, and succeeding as an author.

The astral aspects of my life had continued as well. I saw that my journey wasn't complete, whether I wanted to write about it or not. After accessing several past lives, the lucid dreams didn't stop; instead, I began to enter other realms. I had embarked on astral journeys, seen strange planets, and discussed metaphysical concepts related to the universe with non-terrestrial entities, all guided by Xenex and the Lord of Records.

That afternoon, I found myself once again at a familiar corner cafe. It was only a five-minute walk from my apartment to this coffee shop, which had been my favorite spot for a few years now. It was a special place where I had the freedom to be whatever I wanted. It was also the place where I had taken the time to think through my crumbling marriage before deciding that divorce was the best way to move on with my life.

As I sat there, I observed the melancholy of the few people who had come in for a cold drink. Outside, it felt like an oven. Waves of heat had spread rapidly across Romania—the country was boiling. I was looking forward to writing. Denis was asleep, giving me a few precious moments to be alone and explore other possibilities of existence outside of my current life.

I sat in front of my laptop, listening to music on YouTube, writing about myself and my three-dimensional reality—often a boring routine offering little satisfaction. But I also wanted to write about those magical, touching, and contradictory moments that had challenged me to become who I am now. I wanted to capture what I was feeling and seeing, the person I had become. I wanted to write about those fluctuations within me.

I wanted to describe the times when I felt like I was living in two worlds. The first one was a tangible world, defined by my five senses. It was a world that challenged me to become a fighter in the name of everything that seemed unfair to me. It was a world that inspired me to fight unfairness.

I was also called to write about the second world where there is limitless love, hope, and meaning for what we are doing on Earth. I was inspired to write about that realm where we existed beyond a name written on an identity card. It is a world where I could reinvent and create, where the soul was immortal, and to exist was enough.

My journey as a writer has been strange. As a child, I learned to write small essays in school, which I would perfect with the help of my grandmother. She had written two novels herself, which never saw the light of day. She carried them with her through various homes and through the war, and finally declared it was too late to publish them.

I still have them in a corner of the house, and I remember the surprising perception I had about my grandmother while reading them. I didn't find the firm and tough woman I had known as a child, but a fragile young woman full of emotions whom I could recognize under the mask of the main character. I'm not sure whether I will take on the role of publishing them. At the moment, the project would involve too much time and financial effort, but yes, I carry within me the desire to bring her writing to life.

She inspired me, and in my teenage years, I began writing my first poems. They were painful poems in which I continued to search for something invisible. As an adult, while cleaning the basement, I rediscovered and read some of them. I was shocked by what I found. The past I had recently uncovered was present in these poems. The shadow was present, and the search for the meaning behind it, and the identity of the shadow was palpable. I remembered that after writing these poems, my soul felt lighter. In my current life, I saw that I was trying again to free myself from a past I didn't understand at the time. I smiled.

"What torment," I whispered.

In my youth, I started writing novels at some point. I finished two of them. They were dramatic works of fiction focused on couples. They had a strong psychological bent and were more like theater. As I read my work, my writing seemed strange, with short sentences that almost seemed broken. Emotions seeped through every paragraph. If anyone had tried to read them logically and orderly, the style would have appeared heavy and hard to follow. But if the reader allowed themselves to get carried away and didn't pause at every punctuation mark, the rhythm of reading the book could become exhausting.

After editing the visualizations of my first past life, I realized I had used the same writing style in my first book, a style that was either appreciated or seen as tiring. That style seemed much closer to what I felt as I lived through that experience. At that time, the two earlier novels I wrote were still in draft form on my laptop, and I had no intention of publishing them. Only my mother and a couple of friends had read them.

When I moved to Bucharest, as part of my new life, I started a series of novellas, which I also didn't publish. I had the need to express myself in writing, and I didn't think it was necessary to share what I felt with anyone else. As time went on, I became more confident in what I wanted to write, and I savored every page. It became apparent I was healing myself through writing from an unknown source of sadness.

In 2020, when I received encouragement from my friend Alina to write about my experiences and memories of past lives, it was easy. It was the most accessible way to unload what I was going through. In 2021, I took this a step further as I felt the need to piece together the entire history of my first past life memories. That was also the first time I shared them with people outside my family circle. The encouragement I received from all of them could be summed up in one word: "Publish!"

Then I received the same encouragement from the therapist with whom I first explored the Akashic realm. I came to realize that something beyond my understanding was urging me to publish. I saw there were lots of words of encouragement from people who wouldn't normally be so generous. Finally, through what I initially considered a coincidence—but later recognized as synchronicity—I met someone through a mutual friend who had self-published two novels. She showed me the first steps I could take to self-publish my manuscript.

In 2023, I tested the waters by publishing the first edition of *On the Other Side*. In 2024, I published a second edition after better understanding the self-publishing process. While I feel the decision to publish the first book was entirely mine, I'm not entirely certain that is the case. Was it my choice, or was I inspired by something beyond my understanding?

In the spring of 2024, I began to speculate on passages from my journal that included discussions with Xenex and the Lord of Records. These discussions had a major impact on me. I had the title of my book in mind for some time, but only after seeing the material I had gathered in a seemingly short period did I feel compelled to write and publish a continuation of my spiritual journey. It was strictly my intuition that I was listening to, nothing more. Afterwards, I received encouragement from Xenex, my guide, and several familiar entities I engaged with regularly during my astral travels.

However, the defining moment for me on my publishing journey was the telepathic communication I had one afternoon with the Lord of Records, who clearly told me that much of the information I received was not just for me alone. On the contrary, my duty was to share what I learned with others, one way or another, either alone or with help. The firmness of the message and the direct, yet gentle manner in which it was conveyed to me, clarified that there was no turning back. *Conversation with Xenex* had to be published. The information in the book was not meant solely for me and had to be shared in one form or another.

So, despite the uncertainty I had about how I would publish and my hesitation surrounding how readers might react, I moved forward in the summer of 2024. I realized that what I was doing was an act of trust and faith in all those spiritual communications with non-terrestrial entities I had had over the years.

Was I afraid? Of course. Although I realized I wasn't the only one with extraordinary experiences wanting to share them. I felt like I was setting sail on a sea of unknowns, alone and vulnerable to the potential storm I could be unleashing on myself. Was I really alone on this journey? Or was I still being guided?

Chapter Ten

Lord of Records and Whispers

Now, I heard him whisper in my ear, referring directly to the flight of the storks I was watching through the car window.

"The souls of the storks are not at all different from the souls incarnated in humans. The only difference is that their soul energy is much lighter, simpler in manifestation, and focused solely on the present moment."

I watched them as they spread their wings, preparing for their long journeys ahead. Despite the sweltering 37 degrees Celsius (almost 100 degrees Fahrenheit), I regretted that summer was coming to an end. I would have endured the stifling heat just to enjoy the bright light pouring over nature a little longer. Perhaps a part of me still longed for the warmth of Cuba and a rocking chair. But the Lord of Records didn't allow me much time for daydreaming. He was in the mood to talk. So was I.

"Do you mean that the souls of birds or animals do not possess memory if you say they are focused just on the present moment?"

I couldn't see the Lord of Records visually; I only heard his words forming after the appearance of concepts he flashed to me mentally. I was curious and wanted to challenge him by asking as many questions as possible. I often felt overwhelmed by the information I received from him, and my skeptical mind sought to find errors in his thinking and logic. I cherished his presence. It was as if I was in front of a scholar who could answer all my questions and never lose patience with me.

"They do have memory, of course. Their souls retain significant memories from the past, both pleasant and unpleasant. For example, memories related to survival, traumas, or happy moments. However, the lack of complexity in their consciousness does not drive them to analyze or create hypotheses, as humans do. These souls are not interested in their past or future. They live only in the now, and through human eyes, they may appear much simpler."

As I sat in the car, the whispers of the Lord of Records filled my right ear, like a breeze carrying secrets from another realm. It was one of those happy days when I allowed myself to sit in the passenger seat, which helped me focus on the images swiftly passing by. I was returning from a long trip with my colleague responsible for occupational health and safety. We had visited some of our company's construction sites, and I was relaxed and trying to focus on the moment while my colleague was driving.

It was July, the hottest month of the year. I was paying attention to the storks who had made their nests on the electricity poles. I thought about how different they are from us humans. They have a short life, but it's full of grace. I was lost in admiring the beauty around me. I felt relaxed after an active day. I wanted nothing more than to remain in this state of contemplation.

My communications with the Lord of Records were spontaneous and unexpected. There was no preparation for their occurrence; in a split second, I could feel his presence in my mind, eager to communicate.

This was one of those moments when he was reaching out to connect with me, seeking communication. I heard details about the concepts he was conveying rapidly in my mind, with words connected to images. The words and images blended naturally, allowing me to grasp the essence of what he wanted to tell me, but it was challenging to translate his concepts into words. Sometimes, I could sense his presence with my mind's eye. He usually preferred to contact me during the day, probably because my mind was clearer, and I could focus more easily on the concepts communicated. Along with that, my nights were typically dedicated to astral travels, explorations of the Akashic realm, or communications with—experiencing the spacecraft or being in space as balls of light.

At that moment, I wanted to focus more on what he was conveying to me so that I could remember and transcribe it later. However, my colleague was talkative and occasionally wanted to add something to our languishing conversation. I had fallen into silence several times, and he was confused by my lack of response. I felt obliged to reply to the driver, even as the Lord of Records waited patiently. Usually, such behavior from the Lord of Records indicated that he wanted to convey concepts without much delay.

After answering, I mentally continued my conversation with the Lord.

"Am I to understand that, given their soul energy and consciousness, these souls cannot incarnate and evolve into human or advanced bodies?"

I wondered if there was a distinction between souls based on the simplicity of their manifestation, as he had explained. Or if their existence—in this case as storks—aligned with the Hindu concept that a soul could reincarnate in any chosen form. He was able to perceive my thoughts, so his response came naturally and directly.

"You are mistaken. You are looking at this through a human lens. These souls can indeed evolve. If the consciousness of such a soul—a stork, in this example—wishes to learn more, to undergo new experiences, and to challenge itself, it can choose incarnations in terrestrial or non-terrestrial bodies of more complex beings, in more sophisticated worlds.

"Note that I do not use the term 'more intelligent beings,' as humans are not necessarily more intelligent than the souls of storks. However, human souls have the capacity to express themselves more easily, manifest more readily, and analyze more deeply than animal souls in this world.

"The same applies to organic beings, such as plants, and beyond. Remember, in your first contact with the Akashic Records, you visualized that you had lived lives as crystals or elements of nature. You then realized then that your level of consciousness was the same as it is today; only your modes of manifestation differed from those you have now."

My connection with the Akashic realm was established at the end of 2020, and now I could access it with ease.

After my first experience with the Akasha through regressive hypnosis, I read books that offered sophisticated techniques for accessing the Akashic library. However, I did not practice most of the techniques I read about. They were too formal for my taste and involved preparation rituals and memorizing messages.

In my case, simply formulating the intention and using relaxation techniques allowed me to easily reach this space and ask my personal Book in the Akashic Records ("my Book") about dilemmas, struggles and problems in my daily life that I couldn't understand. I also asked about what the future is likely to hold. I used the time spent in the Akashic space to learn more about my past lives—who I had been and how I became who I am now because of these experiences, and why.

However, it took a long time from when I first accessed the Akashic realm until I connected with the Lord of the Records—the being responsible for the information I could access from my Book. He was the one I asked for permission to access my records each time, but we didn't have direct contact. I only knew he existed in some form in Akasha space, but I never considered that I would have direct communication with him. I had never sensed his presence during my exercise of accessing my Book in Akasha.

I reached this point of direct communication with him in the second half of 2023. It began when I watched several shows on Gaia about how to access someone's Book in the Akashic space. The consent of the person in question was crucial. The show's expert explained how she preferred to contact the Lord of the Records by manifesting the intention of contact while simultaneously asking for the consent of the Lord of the Records responsible for the person whose Book was being accessed.

Whether or not the expert could visualize the Akashic realm, she said she listened carefully to the answers given to her questions. The woman would enter a light hypnotic state and relay word for word what was transmitted to her. The goal was to avoid changing the meaning of what was conveyed. I was impressed by the novelty of the method for accessing the Akashic realm.

What I saw sparked my curiosity and I was interested in experimenting. I wasn't sure whether I wanted to discover more about the Akashic space, or whether I could directly contact my Lord of the Records. I didn't analyze the situation too much; I simply tested it like a child wanting to see what happens when pushing a glass off the edge of the table.

However, I had reservations. Despite all the extraordinary experiences I had in the Akashic space, I remained somewhat skeptical. There remained a part of me that was rational and pragmatic, even though I had gone through extraordinary experiences. Wanting to find an answer, I decided to test the situation. For me, it was all just a huge game of experimentation. I was far from convinced I would succeed. I didn't claim to have the abilities that some people seemed to possess. Still, I felt I had nothing to lose by trying.

Sitting in my car on a beautiful September day in 2023, I toyed with the idea of trying to connect with the Lord of the Records. I was feeling playful and almost convinced that I wouldn't succeed. I was on my way to work, it was a short drive, and I didn't have much time. Ideally, I would have been in a quiet room, alone and well-rested, to attempt this. But that was impossible at home. My son was always there, and in the evenings, I was so tired that I could only consciously visualize and retain spontaneous images.

It seemed somewhat superficial to try to initiate such an important connection during the day while I was by the side of the road. I wondered if I should mentally express my intention to connect. At worst, I wouldn't succeed, I told myself. I decided to give it a try. I pulled the car over and focused on expressing my intention to connect and my desire to communicate with the guardian of my Book.

At first, I felt a presence. Next, there was a voice. I then asked the question I wanted to have answered. At that point, the communication opened up. The communication itself was strange. I had asked about the most likely events that were going to happen by the end of the year. Specifically, I was preoccupied with various daily problems and curious about what the Lord of Records could convey to me. As I wanted to open myself up to whatever guidance the Lord of Records could offer, my questions were not as specific as was typically the case in my Book.

Instead, they were general, allowing him to guide me in envisioning a possible future scenario for the end of 2023. As an answer, I received flashes in the form of images that unfolded very quickly. It was apparent that what I saw were scenes of events and people moving at high speed in front of my eyes. Then, the images would focus on different details. They were like symbols trying to convey something, or rather, they appeared to be metaphors for what might happen. It felt as if all these images were being inserted into my mind with immense force. They overwhelmed me, until I decided to ask for explanations from the presence I felt.

I told the being that it was too much for me and that I was unable to follow along and understand what he was conveying due to the speed the information was being transmitted and the difficulty of understanding the meaning of the metaphors presented. From that moment, I could hear whispers explaining what I was seeing. The information centered around ordinary events in my personal and professional life, rather than significant changes that might occur. However, the manner in which it was transmitted was different. The symbols were exceptional in that they focused on specific details. In particular, two pieces of information appeared repeatedly: the image of me publishing my first book; and the presence of my partner Rico from past lives appearing in my present life.

I chose not to ask questions about Rico's appearance in my current life. It was a recurring theme in much of the information I received about the future. But I had learned from the Akashic space that time was relative, and what I could receive as a certainty that would happen could occur at any time: it could occur in an hour or in several years. I learned the Akasha was not like a fortune teller who would guarantee an event happening at a specific time. Instead, the Akasha suggested the most probable future scenarios if things did not undergo dramatic changes in the life I was living. The same was likely true for Rico.

The second theme was related to the publication of the book. I explained to the Lord of the Records that I had fears about publishing my first book. I knew this self-publication meant a significant financial investment from me, and that I didn't know if I was ready to take that on, along with everything that came with it. In particular, I was reluctant to undertake this project because of the possibility of failure.

I had a deep fear of being without money. Being the head of the family for as long as I could remember and as the one who ensured well-being and comfort, I had this constant pressure of having enough money and managing the household budget. Some of this was due to fears that probably appeared from past life experiences. And my desire to publish my book fell in the category of expensive and unnecessary passions.

Nevertheless, I had begun to take timid steps regarding the self-editing of the manuscript while trying to justify to myself why I wanted to publish it anyway. I had no logical answer for why I wanted to do this. I struggled for many years to keep these experiences secret, and now I wanted to show them to the world and expose myself to criticism. It was then I felt the Lord of the Records whispering to me. It wasn't very clear what he was saying because the whispers mixed with the images. Then I visualized a walnut. It was then he explained what this represented.

"The shell represents the fear of poverty, and the kernel of the walnut represents your peace of mind and sense of security. The shell can be broken with a stone, and the stone is in your hand. Only you can strike the walnut and bring its kernel to light. Only you can overcome your fear and then feel safe beyond it. No one else can do it for you. It is a very common fear on Earth, for all humans."

My feeling was that, in this first contact with the Lord of the Records, our communication had already transformed into that of a master and his student. There was nothing special about what he explained; however, the way he did it was powerful. The image of the walnut itself, the way it cracked open, and the calmness that emanated from his words were like a spell.

I was puzzled as I responded.

"If I conclude that the walnut shell doesn't exist, can I create as much kernel as I need and the type of kernel that is necessary for me?"

The Lord of the Records whispered in reply.

"You can use the form that suits you best."

The communication ended as abruptly as it had begun. I tried for a few seconds to summarize what the Lord of Records had tried to convey to me. He spoke about my fears in various forms, such as the fear of financial insecurity, which impacted how I perceived my new life as a spiritual book author. He also mentioned that this fear could be overcome by me, as the power to break the shell was within me. On the other hand, he reminded me that fear is a common feeling at the vibrational level of the Earth. Although he conveyed a large amount of information in just a few metaphors, it was difficult for me to process it all.

I was shocked after our first communication. Had it really happened? Had I clearly heard and visualized it? Was it just my imagination? But deep inside, I was convinced that something extraordinary had taken place.

Because the communication ended so abruptly, it felt as if it had never existed, and I was keenly aware that I hadn't expressed any intention to end it. It was like someone had disrupted a phone signal. I rejoined the traffic and drove absent-mindedly to work, lost in thought the entire way.

During the communication, I had entered a hypnotic state. My gaze was probably fixed, and to an outside observer, I might have seemed lost in thought. All my concentration was on what I had visualized. The experience was intense, as if I had been connected to an electric wire discharging its energy into my body. I felt slightly euphoric. In the following days, my appetite for testing this new connection grew. My previous contact with the Akasha and the answers to various questions I asked had been exclusively through referencing my Book. Now, I felt the need for a different kind of contact, one that felt more human.

After a few months, the Lord of the Records appeared as a physical presence in our communication. He had a face. He explained to me that the creation of his physical presence was closely tied to my expectations and was in response to some of my needs. Specifically, it was necessary that he be portrayed as a male with certain physical characteristics. These were needs that I could not explain.

The Lord of the Records presented himself as a monk, wearing a long gray robe with a rope belt tied around his waist. He appeared quite young, around 35 years old, with a bald head and a gentle smile on his face. I was confused by this presentation. Why did I perceive him in such an archaic form? Why was his presence solemn and religious when I was neither? These were mysteries.

He clarified this confusion. His appearance was not necessary, but it existed because I had desired a materialization of his presence, and I had a gender preference as well. He explained that he was an androgynous being, an energetic entity. Once again, I heard about the mechanism of intention. And I was told I responded better to certain images and their visualization, according to the Lord of the Records. We discussed this further.

"I am an energetic being," he explained.

"Then why do I perceive you as having a gender? Are you male?" I asked

"It is your choice. Your preference. The need for communication leans towards a preference for gender and appearance."

In the many months that followed, I had numerous communications with the Lord of the Records on various topics, such as energy, parallel universes, the Source, emotions, and more. Over time, our meetings evolved into a regular student-teacher relationship, and his unpredictable way of communicating often surprised me.

There were times when he initiated communication and other times when I approached him through the same mechanism of intention because I wanted to clarify certain metaphysical concepts about the universe. It was, and sometimes still is, difficult for me to keep up with the dynamic ways he explains metaphysical concepts.

The information he provides is a combination of images, symbols, fragments of words, and the use of metaphorical descriptions, all presented simultaneously. Like all people, I need time to decode a combination of concepts presented in diverse forms. Although my mind perceives the meaning, it is challenging to translate it into words and convey all this information in a logical sequence of ideas.

Despite the challenges, I was fascinated by our conversations and the patience with which he would revisit and detail some concepts to make them clearer to me. Usually, I would ask him to accompany me with the respective idea until I was able to access a Word document, confident that I could then transcribe everything he had conveyed to me. During the moments when I transcribed these complex ideas, I developed an automatic, rapid, and confident writing style, through which I managed to capture the essence of everything communicated to me in the shortest time. This communication remains a mystery and a delight for me.

I have no idea how I developed these abilities, such as automatic writing. My mind empties, I try to recall step by step everything I have visualized, heard, or felt, and then I transcribe it. I have always felt guided as I write, even though it seems difficult to convey what I have perceived. Everything happens naturally and effortlessly. It feels as if the information I'm compelled to write is waiting to be expressed.

The discussions I have with the Lord of the Records revolve around cosmic concepts, which are sophisticated even for me. After transcribing them, I often try to verbalize them in conversations, and then I realize that these concepts have been internalized by me when I hear myself speaking about them with naturalness and simplicity.

I am still amazed by my communication with the Lord of Records and sometimes it seems unreal. Still, I cannot explain the clarity and intensity I feel with these communications, along with the automatic writing that accompanies them. Similarly, I don't understand the nature of the abrupt ending of our communication each time.

There is no denying the communications we've had have affected me profoundly. I find them fascinating and often catch myself in discussions with my mother or friends, as I explain complex concepts that I previously discussed with this energetic entity. My role in this communication is interesting too. At the moment of communication, I feel that I am merely a channel through which these concepts are expressed in writing. Yet, upon later reflection, I realize that the information I receive is deeply engraved in my mind.

Still, I have little doubt that I am capable of developing such complex analysis based solely on the limited amount I know about each of these topics. Yet, I feel it is important to acknowledge what I have retained and what I have taken from this spiritual journey.

I have also learned to draw a clear line between my daily life and my spiritual experiments from this ongoing experience with the Lord of the Records. Although his communications can be spontaneous and occur at the most unusual times, I have learned to ask for permission to resume the discussion at a more suitable moment when the time isn't appropriate. These requests are always respected. I also try to connect with him at more convenient times when I want to receive additional details. I have learned it is important for me to focus on only one reality as much as possible throughout the day.

I have also learned a form of communication—and a form of friendship—with this energetic being. I feel as if I am in the presence of a much more learned friend who has graciously dedicated his time to telling me about the universe, even though he realized that many of the complex concepts may escape my understanding at this moment.

I have learned to accept new perspectives on the universe, even if I cannot scientifically prove them. I see them as working hypotheses that I take into consideration as I find similar ideas in specialized literature.

I have also learned the great value of being willing to experiment with new concepts and experiences. There are so many possibilities around us that we refuse to explore out of fear, shame, and the desire not to be judged. There are mysteries within us and around us that want to be discovered, if we only allow them to manifest.

Chapter Eleven

Being a Ball of Light

As a ball of light—an orb—I was fully aware of my individuality, though I didn't place as much importance on it as I did on Earth. I perceived myself as an individual entity, but also as part of everything around me. I knew I was part of the galaxies, cosmic dust, and the void through which I traveled, and it all felt like home. I was part of a whole and had the ability to communicate telepathically with any other form of consciousness. The invisible connection with other life forms was made through invisible cords, which I could sense and recognize as tools to use if I intended to communicate. I was energy, and everything around me was energy too. There were no limits or boundaries; we were all part of the same substance. We were pure energy. Everything and everyone was connected to the same Source.

The Source represents both my beginning and my end. It is my beginning as an individual form of energy as an orb. At the same time, it also represents my end as I merge with it when I returned to being a part of Source. The astral journey as a globe of energy helped me understand that we represented everything and were everything, even though we were just a fragment of an infinite entity.

I was in the car on a late October morning in 2024, driving to a city two and a half hours away from my hometown. I followed one of Romania's national roads, admiring the stunningly beautiful natural scenery, a tapestry of colors ranging from deep green and brown to vibrant yellow. That morning, a thick fog lay over the land, cloaking both forests and open fields in its soft veil. I felt happy—and oddly protected—by this fog.

I was experiencing once again that enchanted moment where the physical, reality-based world as I knew it would transform into an unknown, dreamlike world waiting to be discovered. For a second, I remembered the same sense of mystery and curiosity I had when I began my astral projections. I felt the same sense of anticipation of the unknown, coupled with the desire for total freedom and the urge to know more about the cosmos, about energy, and about what I represent in these astral journeys. I was ready to dive into the world of astral projections.

These astral journeys enchanted me through the sense of well-being they created. It was as if I was discovering myself as a new person for whom the experiences tied to incarnations didn't matter, because I was only energy and existed in a state of bliss and well-being that I could remember when I traveled but couldn't replicate in everyday life. It was a blessing and at the same time a poisoned gift, because I knew that each time it was necessary to return to the daily limitations and petty human struggles.

A few years before, I didn't know much about astral projection, and everything I had read hadn't prepared me for what I was about to experience. My only astral journeys had taken place through my access to the Akashic records and my connection with my Book. I would formulate my question and crystallize my intention to learn more about a particular subject, and then I could experience travel through dimensions without physically moving. This is how I came to explore past lives and possible future scenarios of my life. Over time, I was able to follow my guide, Xenex, to various places. I even surprised him sometimes by initiating contact and reaching the space where he was.

In my repeated attempt to contact Xenex on my own initiative, I discovered ways to travel to new places. During this time, I lost interest in finding out more about past lives in detail. I knew I had innumerable past lives, and even though the lives were complex and exciting and I had had various roles and social positions, I discovered they had the same pattern. I seemed to always live a tumultuous life, constantly in a hurry, which always seemed to end tragically.

After a while, I did not think my past lives had anything more to teach me, and I felt I had to leave them behind me because I had exhausted the topic, and it didn't hold more meaning for me. If I was going to build something in the present, I could do it based on what I had learned from my previous lives, but I needed to break free from the past. I wanted more.

As part of my journey, I discovered that I had existed as a non-terrestrial in other worlds throughout my early incarnations. And in the last non-terrestrial past life, I had decided with my partner, Xenex, to incarnate on Earth. We decided to go on a mission to study human emotions on Earth. The human race had been studied for a long time by his Pleiadian race.

The human race was still a mystery to us in terms of how the environment impacted human decision-making and what role emotions played in making their decisions seemingly radical and unpredictable. It was a mystery how emotions could lead to decisions that were apparently illogical. Furthermore, the human race seemed almost unable to control their emotions. However, it was apparent that human society was built on these emotions, and the Earthlings were a race of survivors exposed to extremes.

From the moment I learned this information, I understood why I had visualized many human lives that were tragic, short, and tumultuous. We both had assumed them for the intense experience of human emotions. Additionally, from my communications with Xenex as my guide, I learned that before incarnating on Earth, he had arranged for his soul's energy to be split: one part would incarnate into a human body and exist on Earth, while the other part would remain in another dimension and act as my guide. The same formula had been applied to my soul, with the difference being that in my human incarnation, I retained most of the energy, leaving only a small part in the other realm. In this way, through that residual energy, we guided each other here on Earth. We each watched over our counterpart and helped guide them.

In my communications with Xenex, I also discovered over time that he held answers to many of my questions, but he wasn't always willing to share them if he felt I wasn't ready. In this regard, he could be a firm and even inflexible guide. Nevertheless, my curiosity was constant and insistent. So, if he didn't initiate contact, I would seek his presence and bombard him with questions. If he didn't want to answer, he would respond vaguely with metaphors, or simply smile.

During these astral journeys through the Akasha realm, I discovered that the symbol on the cover of my Book, which is similar to a compass, could transform into a vehicle for my spontaneous travels. I became used to just touching the symbol on the cover without even opening the Book and then telepathically setting my intention to travel to the desired location. The symbol would light up, and I often felt a burning sensation in my palm resting on the cover.

The steps were always the same and clear. By touching the symbol on the cover, it would light up, seem to detach from the cover, enlarge, and transform into a kind of platform. Using this platform, I could travel. It was enough to reach the space where Xenex was, and the journey happened instantly.

I wanted to fully explore and understand the cosmos, not just see what Xenex showed me. I was already skilled at reaching certain places, but I longed to see the whole universe. I wished to visit the entire universe, but I didn't know how to initiate these general explorations with just my intention. Xenex was reluctant to provide any information about travels beyond the spaces I had known through him and the Book.

Despite my persistent questions about the role of the symbol on the cover of my Book, Xenex always told me it wasn't the right time. I had already experienced our guide-student relationship and knew that he often tried to protect me by deliberately delaying information I wanted to receive as soon as possible. So, I knew I couldn't rely entirely on his support. I was convinced he considered me unprepared and impulsive, taking too many risks to satisfy my curiosity. So again, driven by impulse and curiosity, I decided to try on my own. Because the information I had was incomplete, I could access the desired space only through trial and error.

One night, I decided to experiment with a different approach. I didn't set a clear intention when accessing the Book to reach a specific place; I just wanted to explore the universe, leaving my intention open to any type of experience. The result was surprising.

While I intended to see my guide, the symbol on my Book would typically transform into a platform, and I would find myself almost instantly where Xenex was. This time, however, a tunnel formed in front of me. The tunnel walls appeared to be made of plasma, constantly moving in a circular motion. I could see various particles within it, which I assumed were matrix particles carrying information. The walls were transparent, and through the plasma, I could observe the cosmos.

The further I advanced through the tunnel, the faster the plasma seemed to move in a circular motion from my left to my right. This circular motion of the plasma formed the tunnel. When I touched the walls, they felt like they were made of a material that was viscous, somewhere between liquid and solid.

Through the walls, I could clearly see the universe with stars and galaxies, but as I progressed, the universe appeared increasingly distorted, and the image beyond the walls became unclear until it was impossible to perceive. In the end, I only saw two colors—gray and white—forming the walls. I assumed the transparent nature of the walls disappeared as the plasma's speed increased around me.

During my journey through the tunnel, I felt a strong and firm force pushing me from behind, as I ejected out of the tunnel. I later learned that this force could vary in intensity, sometimes stronger, sometimes weaker. While traversing the tunnel, I perceived myself in a humanoid form, but upon exiting, I saw I was transformed into a glowing energy orb. At no point did I fear for my safety. Instead, I felt an overwhelming sense of liberation and joy, similar to what a child feels when coming upon an elaborate playground. The sensation was overwhelming, and nothing could add to my state of bliss. It was a feeling of fulfillment, happiness, and calm that I rarely experienced in my life.

Over time, I learned about the infinite abilities I possessed in this form. I had 360-degree vision, even though there was no organ or known means by which I could see externally. As an energy orb, I could travel at incredibly high speeds, and like a spaceship, I could stop or change my speed at will. Distances between galaxies could be traversed in what I perceived as seconds.

In my orb form, I had the ability to decide, feel, and act far more freely than I ever could as a human. In that state, I didn't feel the need for a physical body. I felt free to move and take action without the limitations of a physical form.

I discovered my vision, hearing, and sense of touch were tested during these astral journeys, and they had the same characteristics as my human senses. They functioned in the way that I was familiar with in my human form. As for smell and taste, I had an indication of their existence, but they were far from the sensations we know as humans.

These senses seemed muted, allowing me to identify smells and tastes, but without the pleasure of savoring them. In other words, I knew what they were and could identify them through telepathic images, but I couldn't experience them in a human way. I had the same experience during my astral travels near Xenex. Sometimes, I could identify his characteristic scent and recognize it through images, but I couldn't breathe it in naturally as I would on Earth.

Interestingly, the emotions I felt had the intensity I knew in human form. However, they vibrated at a higher frequency, so that I only felt joy, happiness, love, and empathy. I didn't feel negative emotions like fear, worry, or anger in the astral plane. The absence of these negative feelings made the experience incredibly uplifting. The sense of liberation I felt while moving as an energy orb through the universe was infinite. There were no limitations or forbidden aspects during these travels. I perceived this cosmic space as familiar and safe.

There were also moments when I could observe other orbs, other souls, moving in a similar way to how I traveled as an energy orb. I wanted to study the universe around me and closely observe celestial bodies. Through intention, I could decide to stop near any cosmic body and land on solid surfaces, whether they were planets or other celestial bodies, such as a comet or a moon, if I wished. This could even include visiting a star. I could exist near one as a glowing orb without my energy form being affected in any way.

There was no specific form of communication with the other energy spheres or orbs in the way we understand communication in a human sense. It was as if we transmitted frequency waves between us, sharing our states of well-being and perceiving those of the others. The spheres had no names, and I couldn't identify them as people I knew or those who had died. Yet, they all represented my greater family. We knew each other beyond human conventions and were energetic parts of one another.

My focus in this form of light and energy was to study and observe other forms of consciousness, similar to mine or not, and to simply enjoy my existence in this wonderful dimension. I discovered within myself a desire to play. The energy orbs would play with each other or even form play groups. It might seem strange and comical that an astral consciousness would be interested in play. However, through play, the bond between different souls was strengthened, and the abilities of each form of consciousness were tested. More than once, I was involved in this cosmic dance, which could involve activities like racing around cosmic bodies using speed as the primary ability, or playing a game like tag, where the goal was to energetically chase and touch other orbs of light.

Of course, my guide Xenex recognized my astral travels and advised me to be cautious in how I launched these astral projections. He telepathically transmitted the image of the cord connecting my energy form to my body and how this connection could potentially be severed if I wasn't careful. Breaking the cord would lead to the complete abandonment of my human body and inevitably to its death if my astral adventure took me to places from which I didn't know how to return.

Despite the severity of the consequences if I lost my connection, I felt no sense of fear during these journeys, nor was I worried about the possibility of detaching from the cord. I somehow intuitively realized that this cord would only detach if I decided so and if my intention was directed toward such an action. Was there temptation in these astral journeys? Of course there was. The state of well-being and happiness I experienced made returning difficult. The longer I remained in my energetic form, the less I wanted to be tied to a human body and return.

However, I always remembered my anchor in everyday life, which was my mother and my little boy. I realized if there was one precaution I had to take, it was related to myself and what I desired. Spending a longer period in the form of an energy sphere gradually, in my case, diminished the desire to exist in an incarnated form, no matter what that form might have been. As a result, I felt afterward that it was harder for me to return to my body.

There were moments when I could even see the cord as a thread of light trailing behind me as I moved through the tunnel during my journeys. From my communications with Xenex and the Lord of Records, I understood that maintaining this state for an extended period is linked to the soul's detachment from the body, thereby dissolving the connection to the terrestrial plane where I am incarnated. In short, it could cause the physical body's death if the soul remains absent for too long.

I believe that sustaining such a form on the astral level could indeed lead to the soul's detachment from the body, simply through my own intention. There were moments when the emotions of happiness were so strong inside me that I didn't want to return to my Earthly plane. I think this is what Xenex referred to as abandoning the human vessel. However, there is a prohibition against continuing this process because of that very reason and there is a pressure to separate from this form imposed by an external force. The very contracts the soul has assumed through incarnation, along with the mission the soul has set for itself, require the being to be present in the physical dimension. In my case, this meant staying with my body on Earth.

At first, I didn't understand Xenex's reluctance to restrict my astral travels, especially right after I had developed a taste for them. However, I respected his request due to the seriousness with which he presented it. He also added that using the symbol on the cover of my Book during these astral travels would leave energetic traces throughout the universe, traces that could be easily identified by other beings. His concern was that I was not just an energy being but an entity leaving a body during my astral travels, and it was necessary to return to that form. He was worried that I was exposing myself to unnecessary risks, making me vulnerable to the unknown.

The risk centered around coming into contact with energetic frequencies I didn't know, and which could, intentionally or unintentionally, cause harm. At the same time, due to my existence in the three-dimensional plane, I was exposed to encountering entities on the same frequency who might not have my well-being at heart. Xenex conveyed this information to me telepathically. What he most often requested was that I exercise caution and conduct my exploration in his presence.

Convinced by my impetuousness, my overwhelming desire to learn, and my curiosity to continue these astral journeys, he indicated another symbol which would not necessarily allow my energetic imprint to be identified. He indicated the symbol I could use to launch these astral travels was the Star of David. I didn't receive an explanation as to why this symbol was better or what special characteristics it had. Nevertheless, I followed his advice, and I made my new astral journeys using the new symbol, and only when I was in Xenex's or Rico's energetic presence.

In this way, I was able to experience the most extraordinarily intimate activity between two beings. It occurred when two energy orbs, two souls, decided during play to collide and merge into a single orb. It is difficult to explain the origin of this particular desire, but the emotion evoked by this moment surpassed any human experience I've ever had. I liken it to soul's initial merging with the Source—a return to the beginning when the soul was united with the very essence that granted it independent existence.

This was an act of utmost importance, extreme intimacy between souls, and a deliberate choice of which energy orb or soul another soul wished to merge with. I sensed that this kind of experience was deliberate, and it didn't happen with just any energy orb. Souls had preferences for other souls they knew better, were closer to, and shared the same level of development with. However, this didn't exclude the possibility of different souls wanting to experiment with more distant souls, with whom the degree of familiarity was not as high.

Although the desire for this union into a single orb resembles the soul's longing to be one with the Source, the soul never ceases to exist outside the Source. The soul's consciousness never leaves the Source; this separation from Source is merely an illusion. This poses the question of how a soul's consciousness can perceive its existence both within and outside the Source?

I now understand the soul experiences this separation through the perception of its own created reality, which is nothing more than a holographic projection where the soul's consciousness experiences different lessons. In this case, it is more than just a connection between the soul and the Source. Ultimately, the soul never leaves the Source, it just has the impression that this separation takes place.

The desire to merge between two souls, in my case, was limited to experiencing union with the energy orb of my constant partner Xenex (Rico) from multiple terrestrial or non-terrestrial lives. The connection was much deeper than that of two partners, friends, or anything experienced in a guide-student relationship, and this was mirrored on the astral level. Our relationship was so intimate that in the astral space I could recognize his energy orb without any physical indication that it was him. I sensed his energetic imprint every time I was near his presence.

Each energy orb has a unique imprint and an unmistakable vibrational level. Sometimes, on the surface of the orb, one can observe continuous moving striations that show the shape and color of the waves according to which that energy functions. Another characteristic of energy orbs is the color each orb possesses. The shade of the color is also part of each soul's imprint. I couldn't say whether the color itself represents a level of soul development or is just a preference. Communication between souls in the form of energy orbs occurs telepathically. Information and emotions are transmitted through images, thoughts, and emotions, with communication occurring in a very concentrated form.

When we decided to experience the first union of our energy orbs, this union led to a collision that caused an explosion similar to an atomic reaction, resulting in the formation of a single orb. Although we became One, each of us retained our individual consciousness within the energy orb we had formed. We could perceive ourselves as separate consciousnesses. The individual colors of our orbs mixed but did not form a new shade. Instead, the surface of the orb displayed patches of different colors.

During this time, we were able to communicate telepathically with each other. The act itself was much more intimate than any previous telepathic communication. It was almost as if we were not communicating but simply knowing that we were part of the same whole, with our thoughts intertwined. It was difficult to describe the sensation during this union. It was a state of happiness and ecstasy unmatched by anything I've ever known.

Unfortunately, we could not maintain this combined orb form for a long period. The form changes from an orb to a spiral, with the two energies of different colors forming something very similar to strands of intertwined DNA. Somehow, we knew that in this new form, we could exist forever without wanting to separate from each other.

However, something external prevented us from maintaining these forms for a longer time. It felt like a wave of energy, a force that compelled us to separate and return to our original humanoid forms. No matter how much we wanted to maintain this form, our insistence on not separating ended with us being thrown through the same tunnel but in the opposite direction, eventually connecting us to our physical reality.

Ultimately, these astral journeys took me to realms I don't think I fully understood. I visualized dimensions where the objects and beings I saw were holograms, which I could modify by manipulating their pure energy. At first, I thought it was another existential plane functioning in this format, and I was merely an observer. Then I realized that I was the creator of this holographic world, and this ability to create belonged to any energy orb, not just me. However, even here, there were preferences. Each soul consciousness, each energy orb, could have preferences about what they created, how they created it, and how advanced or simple these creations were. It was also the soul's decision whether to bring their creation to life or not.

Creation is brought about by using pure energy particles, each of which possesses its own consciousness. However, when these energy particles are used to form a new entity, they must unify into a single, collective consciousness. The moment these particles merge into one unified awareness, the form is considered alive.

Creation could be initiated simply by a soul expressing its intention and then shaping the consciousness of pure energy. The possibility of a creation to take form and come into life was limitless and ultimately depended more than anything else on the soul's ingenuity and the confidence it had in its creation. Through the process of creation made by a soul, the pure consciousness energy can be transformed into something new. In this new form of existence, the energy could learn new lessons through its new form. Pure consciousness energy in its original form does not have the need to learn. It could just exist in a latent state before deciding to take a particular form by an act of soul's creation.

These astral journeys also made me wonder: what did these holographic spaces represent? Could they have been my incarnations as a non-terrestrial entity, in an energy form from a higher frequency plane in a completely different universe? Or did they truly represent the initial form of the soul's consciousness, the pure form, which could later choose incarnations in various denser planes of holographic existence?

I am inclined to give more credit to the latter option. I considered all these visualizations as expressions of my purest existence near the Source, without any connection to having a physical body or a known system of existence. In this form, my soul was testing the process of creation and the complete freedom of being, reminding me of what I truly am. Despite all these incredible experiences, I'm still not sure how I was able to access and experience this form of existence on the astral plane.

The end result is that my experiences during astral journeys enriched me spiritually. I discovered that when I exist without constraints or limitations—living in a state of bliss and happiness—I enter one of the most beautiful states I have ever experienced in my entire life. The desire to exist in this energetic form on another plane, without any kind of barriers, encourages me to get out of bed in the morning when I struggle to find meaning in my physical life.

Another aspect that moved me deeply is the connection I felt with the other energy spheres. I existed in an energetic form, bathed in an atmosphere of love, tolerance, and safety in which there was no trace of judgment, rejection, or doubt. I existed simply to exist, not to prove to others or to myself that I am enough. I lived in that state of acceptance of everything that surrounded me.

Perhaps the most intense aspect which impacted me as a person was the unparalleled act of union between two energy spheres. The sensation of fulfillment and security I could feel by being part of the other and yet still retaining my individuality cannot be compared to the human terms we use for the act of love. I believe the same sensation can only be equaled by merging with the Source and becoming one.

The positive emotions and feelings I discovered during these journeys are extraordinarily profound. I try to integrate what I have learned and felt, in one form or another, into my everyday life.

Chapter Twelve

The Bottle and Parallel Universes

In November 2023, I became used to my communication with the Lord of the Records. Despite the novelty wearing off regarding the way our communication took place, the concepts presented to me were exotic, intriguing, and surprising.

However, despite my fascination with our discussions, there were many moments when the rational reality-based part of my mind wanted to downplay or ignore what had been shared with me. In particular, I struggled to assimilate the concept of parallel universes. The mere thought that a part of my consciousness could exist in many places at the same time was difficult to accept. Furthermore, the concept that I exist in much more comfortable and quiet forms of existence filled me with disbelief. That last part was especially challenging.

I kept questioning why I was not more aware of those "more comfortable" universes and why I had to fend for myself as I navigated the challenges of this universe where I was consciously living. I later grasped that I misunderstood this concept. I had ignored that these parallel universes existed only as perceptions of holograms to intensify the lessons of a soul, and that time did not exist as we perceived it on Earth. Still, there were many times when I asked the Lord of the Records for proof of what he was explaining to me. I wanted evidence that my five senses could understand, based on the measures I used in my everyday life. I wanted more clues and explanations for these metaphysically sophisticated concepts but based upon the system I understood.

That same month, in 2023, it seemed like everything was converging to provide me with information about what I was refusing to accept. That autumn, I was invited to a human resources business conference at a Ramada hotel in Sibiu, my hometown. It was a networking event with suppliers in the human resources field, and at the same time, I was participating in a panel interview where we discussed changes in the labor market. I wasn't a fan of such events, but I accepted the invitation to push myself out of my shell and connect with people in my chosen field. Outside of my everyday life, I was experiencing too many unexplained phenomena, so I felt an infusion of reality based on tangible numbers wouldn't have hurt. Additionally, my friend Gaby was giving a presentation and wanted me there to provide encouragement and support.

I am naturally an introvert, although this trait isn't always visible in my daily life. People often tell me that I create an invisible barrier around myself that can't be crossed unless I allow it. In those moments, I retreat into my shell and just want to be left alone. Since embarking on this path of spirituality, my need for isolation has grown. Previously, I felt the need for others and reached out to them, but after my recent metaphysical experiences, I found I could remain alone without any sorrow. In this way, I let others seek me out if they wished.

Despite my natural inclination to avoid contact, I spent the entire day at this event. I arrived early and was able to choose a seat at a table right in front. I wanted to be as close to the stage as possible so I could follow Gaby's presentation. I knew she had been quite stressed, and we had talked on several occasions about her topic of how to do employer branding when there's no allocated budget. I smiled when I thought about the subject. Gaby had decided to be bold and get straight to the point. The vast majority of HR managers in Romania were dealing with small or nonexistent investment budgets, and employer branding was still seen as a luxury.

My next wish was to drink some water. For a year, I had been on a diet, and for most of the day, water was the only liquid I consumed. To stay alert and engaged, it was crucial to ensure I had enough water with me. Before the presentation started, I brought two bottles of water to my table. I opened one and began drinking it. The other was placed next to the first bottle, on the table, in front of my seat.

The round table where I sat was also occupied by four gentlemen. I didn't know them, but the table was large enough to allow ample personal space, even if we chose not to introduce ourselves. Once the presentations began, my attention shifted to the stage. During this time, there was no movement in the room—no one stood up from our table or the neighboring ones, and the waiters did not enter the room. Neither I nor the four people at the table made any move.

After 15 minutes, I noticed the water level in my bottle was decreasing, even though I hadn't taken a single sip. I then looked over at the second bottle. To my surprise, it was no longer in front of me. The bottle was not on the table. For a moment, I was in shock. Where had the bottle gone? Mentally, I reviewed my actions and how I had acquired the bottles. I had indeed taken two bottles of water from the bar and placed them to my right, and in those 15 minutes, no one from our table had moved.

I was confused. What could explain the disappearance of the bottle? I searched for an explanation, no matter how absurd. I then checked the number of water bottles in front of the gentlemen at the table. The simplest explanation was that one of them had taken my bottle. But how had I not noticed? My peripheral attention is excellent, and I easily observe everything happening around me. I calmed down, considering it a mistake, and assumed my table companions didn't know the bottle belonged to me.

Soon after, I decided to get up during the conference and left the room. I took a new bottle of water from the bar and placed it in front of me again. My attention turned to the conference stage for a few minutes because Gaby was presenting. But this time, I was on alert. I looked at the table again shortly after. There was the empty bottle I had finished, the second opened bottle I had taken from the bar a few minutes earlier, and a third sealed bottle. It appeared to be the exact bottle I had just been looking for and couldn't find. It was the same brand of still water, a sealed bottle placed in the same spot, and it was very close to me—about 20 centimeters away.

Again, I was in shock. Where had the bottle come from? When I returned from the bar, there was only the empty bottle on the table, but after a few minutes of focusing on the stage, the missing bottle had reappeared. It was as if someone was playing tricks on me. I looked at it many times and tried to understand where it had come from. Despite going through mental gymnastics as I considered all logical possibilities, I was unable to provide myself with an explanation for what I had witnessed. An object that existed, then disappeared, and reappeared within forty-five minutes could not have a logical explanation. Rather, it was completely illogical.

Then I remembered my discussions about parallel universes with the Lord of the Records. What I had witnessed represented a jump from one parallel universe to another, and the way to identify this jump was through details that could easily change, such as the existence or absence of a water bottle. I also remembered discussing the existence and nature of parallel universes with the Lord of the Records and how I had insisted on receiving proof from him. Was this the proof I had been looking for?

I then wondered what impact the presence or absence of a water bottle on the conference table could have on my universe.

Could this detail completely alter my existence in the new parallel universe I had accessed? Could my life be so different just because of a water bottle? Could I discover that my relationships with people in my life were different? Maybe I was still married? Maybe my job had different responsibilities? What I knew was that during the short period of about 45 minutes, in which I made this jump between existences, I didn't feel any different from usual.

There was no panic on my part; I calmly accepted things as they were. I had simply chosen to live in the present, with everything that this moment brought me.

Why I made the jump back, or why I rediscovered the bottle, is hard to explain. Maybe it was because I had asked for proof, and the disappearance and reappearance of the bottle showed me that something extraordinary had happened. I knew it wasn't the first time such a phenomenon had happened to me. But that day was the first time I had admitted this type of occurrence could be a jump between two parallel universes. It was also the first time I had closely followed what had happened and couldn't offer any other logical explanation for everything that had occurred.

The bottle had clearly appeared and disappeared. In the past, there were situations where, for a few seconds while driving home from work, I had the sinking feeling that when I got home, I would find a different house with more family members than when I had left for work that morning. I was so sure of this—even though my logical mind contradicted it—that I crossed the threshold of the house feeling excitement, anticipation, and curiosity, expecting to find something different. It was a profound emotion, totally indefensible from a logical point of view, and it annoyed me.

I wondered, "Is it possible to create or be in the reality I desired in those few seconds?" However, the sensation would disappear after a few moments, before I arrived home. The sensation was strange. My logical mind was present, telling me that nothing had really changed in my reality. However, I felt as if I were temporarily existing in another universe—very similar to the familiar one, but with certain elements that were different. These phenomena repeated several times without any apparent explanation.

They were seconds that enriched me spiritually through the fullness of the emotion I felt. I felt the excitement of having the possibility for a few moments to be another me in another universe. It was a world full of new possibilities, where my choices had been different. It sparked my curiosity. The moments were spontaneous, appearing and disappearing in the same way. The common aspect of all these occasions was the high degree of relaxation I felt and the fact that I was focused only on the present and nothing more.

After the episode with the disappearing and reappearing water bottle, during my next communication with the Lord of the Records, I insisted that he explain more about the concept of parallel universes and how it functions. His explanation came in his characteristic style—visual and metaphorical. I saw a network resembling a neural network, with thinner and thicker threads branching off a main trunk. The image looked like a tree.

"...these luminous branches, similar to cables, are the realities in which you are present. The threads branching off from the main trunk are the various parallel worlds and life scenarios you can have through a physical manifestation and/or in a plane of existence."

What I concluded from my communication with him was that I am present in all these realities, similar to a tree or neural branches, at the same time, but I am only conscious of one universe. Some realities were more likely to happen, with bigger branches, while others were weaker, with very thin branches. He also insisted that the jump from one universe to another is not distinctly felt by us as individuals. We can only observe this jump by the change of some minor details that later have a major impact on the reality we are aware of.

My questions continued.

"Why is a universe not felt differently from another?"

Further, I asked him why are we only consciously aware of one reality? Why are we consciously present in only one parallel universe and not in multiple ones?

The Lord of the Records explained that due to the dense vibrational plane we live in, it is almost impossible for a human being to consciously perceive the existence of multiple realities.

"Humans still lack the capacity to understand such concepts and to detach from their earthly existence. This doesn't mean that this information doesn't exist within them. All this knowledge is there, but humans don't yet know how to access it. Energy beings are most familiar with these concepts and can easily access multiple realities simultaneously. The consciousness of existing in parallel in multiple places and realities can be easily assimilated by these beings without impacting their consciousness structure."

Again, I concluded that due to the density level at which we live on Earth, our consciousness, with our human mind residing in a physical body, cannot easily rise to the vibration level where it could experience different realities. It is hard for the human mind to accept the concept and integrate it into its belief system. However, the knowledge has always existed in the DNA of the soul.

Admittedly, my interest in this subject was somewhat selfish. I was interested in learning what I could choose and how I could select the parallel universe I desired. Could

I choose a plane of existence that was much easier and closer to what I wanted? If these jumps were possible, how could I reach and stay in my preferred reality? And if it was possible, how could I do it immediately?

The Lord of the Records responded calmly and warmly.

"There is no need for anything. You are being shown various proofs that parallel universes exist, and you just need to pay attention to what you experience. Beyond that, you just need to live in the present. Be present in your present. Nothing more."

At that moment, I had confirmation that the proof of the existence and non-existence of the water bottle on that table at the conference had been facilitated by him to convince me of the essence of our conversations and that these conversations with the Lord of Records had undoubtedly taken place. While I didn't have reason to doubt these conversations had occurred, I always approached these discussions with him from a logical, critical mindset. I still insisted on understanding how I could connect with the reality I desired.

I telepathically asked the Lord of the Records for clarification again. The response was clear.

"...you were simply present in the moment. Nothing more is needed. How do pain, trauma, and fear manifest? Through thoughts. What do these thoughts do? They transport you to the past and future, to the hypothetical. Then you are not present in the here and now, you are elsewhere. When you connect with the present and stay in it, you can connect with most of your energy and thus access those branches (of the tree you saw) that lead you to another scenario of reality, to another parallel universe. Being present connects you with yourself, with your energy, and allows you to manifest another preferred reality. Be present."

The concept of being present wasn't new. It was a popular mindset among those who wanted to implement change in their lives and manifest everything they desired. But what did it mean to be present? Did it mean existing outside of an imagined future and living only with what appeared in our lives? Letting ourselves be surprised? Did it mean not creating strong connections with those around us, thinking that being present means living with those around us only in the moment without trying to impact the future? I couldn't understand and assimilate a present where I didn't harbor a personal prediction about what would happen or a thought about a future plan. What did this call to "live in the present" mean?

Why was this jump from a less satisfactory universe to a more desired universe done just by being present? Was it that by being present and focusing on small details, I could live my life by being aware of the details around me, which could guide me toward making different choices? Or was it because I could use my intention as a tool to create the version of reality where I wanted to live? The inescapable conclusion was that my soul could find more ways to manifest, despite my mind trying to guide me based on past experiences or future catastrophic scenarios.

I received the answer shortly after, on a beautiful and warm winter day. It was December, and the holiday season was approaching. It was the time of year that reminded me of childhood, the sound of the pestle as my grandmother ground sugar, the smell of walnuts and homemade chocolate, and walking with my mother through the city markets in search of a Christmas tree to bring home.

Now I was in the car again, heading to work in the afternoon. In the afternoon, I would pick up my son from kindergarten, leave him at home with my mother, and then return to the office. Sometimes, those were the most peaceful moments of my day. I was lucky to live close to my workplace. On this day, the sunlight was incredibly bright on the street, illuminating everything it touched in its warm, radiant light. In an instant, spontaneously, I felt so happy to BE, to EXIST, at that moment, here and now. There was no specific reason for this happiness. It was a day like any other, and I didn't anticipate anything extraordinary happening. Yet the happiness was overwhelming and wasn't connected to anything I had done or was about to do. It wasn't linked to any action of mine or a possible benefit. I was simply happy to exist.

This reaction in the moment seemed extraordinary to me. My existence in this ethereal winter light seemed to transform everything around me; it was the light in which I felt I was gaining unexpected powers. Anything seemed possible at that moment, and yet nothing in my existence seemed logically important enough to have prompted the well-being I felt. This sense of well-being faded after a few dozen minutes when I started working on the tasks I had to complete at the office. It wasn't long before the bliss I had experienced faded into the background. There were still traces of happiness in me, but my mind was fixed on the future and what I had to achieve, leaving the beauty of the light I had been bathed in lingering somewhere behind me.

I often wondered what happened that afternoon. What did I feel and what did I connect with? There was a brief period when it seemed like a veil was created between my current reality and the thoughts that tied me to the past. The emotions I learned in that past, and the thoughts I harbored about an uncertain future were completely removed from my awareness. I managed to connect only with the present. I connected with what I was in my essence, beyond just being a body and acting out a role. I was simply ME. That ME was beyond everything that existed in my physical reality. At that moment, everything I experienced was just in the NOW.

At the end of 2024, I started a discussion about parallel universes with Haris, my ex-husband. He had changed, and without realizing it, we approached the subject of spirituality. He had embraced spirituality without me knowing and was reading quite a few books on the topic. We were relaxed with each other and were testing what each of us was learning about spirituality. I told him about my story with the water bottle, and he offered his opinion.

"You can indeed change your perception of a certain thing, action, or person, and thus your life can take a different course and most likely exist in another parallel universe. However, you cannot change the past and the actions of the past. Take our case, for example. You can change your perception of our divorce, but you cannot change the action itself, the divorce."

I smiled when I heard this. These were concepts I had considered many times and discussed with the Lord of the Records in my insistence on finding answers. I replied.

"In the context where time does not exist, and the past and future are in the NOW, a change in what happens now will alter both dimensions of time as we know them. The change itself accesses another parallel universe through a jump from the NOW. If the jump is significant enough,

I don't think we will remember the past as we knew it before. We will perceive the past differently, and it will exist differently. Why won't we remember what has changed? Because, as human beings, we are incapable of consciously accessing more than one parallel universe. Thus, the change in perception will impact how you perceive your past and will reshape your recollections so that they are no longer like they were previously."

After the discussion with my ex-husband, I tried to analyze whether the words and ideas I expressed were mine, representing the essence of my conversations with the Lord of the Records, or if it was him speaking through me. Beyond that specific conversation, the clarity with which I could describe and explain sophisticated concepts often surprised even me. I still don't have an answer. However, there are moments when I feel guided to write certain paragraphs.

The essence of what I told my ex-husband was that if he is capable of accessing one parallel universe that is quite different from the present universe he inhabits, he will not be able to remember the previous one. There will be a total cut-off from the last universe, and the past will be reshaped.

In the end, I recalled one of my astral journeys with the help of the Book and the tunnel I had traveled through, floating in the universe as an energy orb. This time, there was a black hole before me. I slipped through the hole as energy and felt as if I had reached a completely different universe. It was strange that I knew this information without receiving it from anyone. I saw from a distance the black hole I had passed through was the meeting point of the two parallel universes. These parallel universes communicated with each other at certain points through these black holes. Visually, I could compare these parallel universes to onion layers. They overlapped with each other and were separated by a very thin layer, almost impossible to penetrate without the existence of a passage like the black hole.

I don't claim to fully understand this concept of parallel universes, but what I have gathered from these conversations is that we, as humans, live simultaneously in multiple realities. We navigate between them throughout our lives, often without realizing it. However, we can pay attention to various inconsistencies throughout the day and even the emotions we feel within our environment. These can indicate subtle or profound changes that we cannot logically explain. This could also be an indicator that the universe we perceive is a different one.

I also understand that when we change our perspective on what surrounds us, it can result in a jump to another parallel universe that aligns with our new perspective or approach. The most important thing in determining which universe we live in is how each of us positions ourselves in the reality where we currently exist.

Perhaps the most perplexing point is that despite all the knowledge of this concept of parallel universes, the message from the Lord of the Records was clear. We live in holographic realities that our soul has chosen to experience, and in this case, nothing we experience in this learning environment is real. It is merely created based on what we have focused upon. Our creation belongs to each of us through the mechanism of intention. The extent to which we can give birth to our desired intention and create a manifestation we consciously choose depends on each of us.

All this information overwhelmed me at some point. My takeaways from these experiences revolve around three concepts.

First, my intentions and focus are more important than anything else in creating my reality. Existing in a holographic world created by myself for myself, I have the possibility to make a choice at any time—through the mechanism of intention—toward another reality that is more desirable to me. I understand there is no such thing as karma or destiny, unless I choose to believe in it. If that is my focus and it guides my reality, I will be aware of evidence that confirms my beliefs.

Another lesson I learned is about how I can feel excited when I remember that I also exist in a universe other than the one I know as my current reality—the one that I am conscious of. I realized that I have access to a universe that exists at a higher vibrational level, and my feeling of happiness and calm comes precisely from that vibrational level.

Another takeaway from my experiences is the demonstration of undeniable proof surrounding the existence of parallel universes. My conversation with the Lord of Records centered upon my need for proof showed me this. I am always amazed that the proof he provides for this information eventually comes—perhaps not when I expect it, but it does arrive. As a result, I feel safe and seen by him, and I sense that our conversation has a much deeper purpose than I can fully grasp. I feel this way because I know I am in contact with an entity who patiently listens to me and dedicates his time and energy to explaining complex and important aspects of the universe to me.

Chapter Thirteen

Premonition, Paranormal Events and Back to My Old Reality

My second book, *Conversation with Xenex*, was released at the end of 2024, and as the year drew to a close, I realized I was suffering from chronic fatigue and restlessness. It had been a busy and productive year. I had launched two books, worked on interesting projects at my job, faced challenges from my son—who oscillated between moments of remarkable maturity and the tantrums of a two-year-old—completed business coaching school, and reached a more balanced relationship with my ex-husband. Looking back at 2024, I saw many reasons to be proud of myself. Yet, something inside me hinted that the last two months of the year would bring turbulence.

Suddenly, I noticed white spots on my son's fingernails, reminding me of the calcium deficiency I had suffered as a child. I also had white spots under my nails and a craving to eat walls because of stress, anxiety, or my calcium deficiency. I had even indulged this craving by tasting the exterior wall of our balcony.

Because of my personal experience, I decided to have a complete set of blood tests done to check his overall health. My intuition told me he needed a thorough check-up as soon as possible. When the results came in, I discovered that three indicators were outside the normal range and could point to health problems. One was related to blood sugar and another to liver health. Blood sugar issues were quite familiar to me. Both my mother and grandmother had developed diabetes as they aged, and my ex-husband was also showing signs of the condition. I knew the issue well. But he was a small boy. How could Denis develop something like early diabetes? I was devastated.

In an instant, I felt my world crumble and nothing else mattered. I spent an entire day moving like an automaton, trying to think of how I could solve a potential problem that had no solution. I am action oriented, and I felt at that moment that I had been denying this important part of me. All the consciousness elevation undergone in recent years regarding the role of spirituality in my life and all the experiences that helped me accept my present reality and understand the facets of the universe faded away. Everything else seemed irrelevant when confronted with a threat to the health and safety of my little boy. This panic I felt could not be soothed by the thought that there must be a soul plan behind these challenges in this version of reality, or that everything happens for a reason.

I suddenly remembered that I had received signs about the possibility that Denis might have a health issue. I had a dream that warned me about it. At the same time, I realized that throughout my life, I had experienced events whose meaning I couldn't explain. I had received signs through dreams—premonitions that, years ago, I had chosen to ignore. But now, because of everything I had been through, I had a completely different perspective. This chapter is about the signs that revealed themselves to me through dreams. It's also about some of the inexplicable events I've experienced.

These experiences are not unique to me; most of us have likely encountered something similar. That's why understanding these signs might also matter to you. As you reflect on your life, it's very likely that each of you has experienced at least one event that defied logical explanation, something that has stayed with you ever since. In this chapter, I explore possible explanations for such events in my life and draw parallels between what I perceived in dreams and what unfolded in my reality.

Specifically, on that day with my son, I remembered a dream I'd had a few days earlier. I dreamt I was standing on an airfield. I was alone and holding my son's hand. At that moment, I saw a huge ship, shaped like a rocket, with no visible propulsion system, landing in the middle of the field. The white and red colors painted on the ship's outer shell attracted me, yet its appearance also filled me with fear and suspicion. Was it a non-terrestrial ship or a human one? It was all very confusing. I couldn't even understand why I was asking myself this question. Beyond that, I didn't understand what it was doing here, in this place, and why was the ship landing so close to us? Why were we in this place, here and now?

While I was dreaming, I vaguely remembered being in a similar place before. I recalled seeing it in another dream. There was a similar ship, but I couldn't remember what happened afterward. In real life, I had never been to such a place or seen a launch. As the ship landed, I saw people coming out. They were dressed in tight protective suits and were wearing helmets similar to those of astronauts, but they were much more discreet.

They indicated that I should move towards a huge hangar behind us. Following their instructions, I found other families in the hangar. The hangar turned out to be a kind of factory producing chemicals, but not the ones known to us civilians. We were told that everyone in the hangar had been irradiated and needed to be injected with a certain substance. They didn't provide details about what the substance was. I remember being somewhere at the back of this immense hall, which had glass walls through which the airfield could be seen. Next to me was an older woman who seemed to be a nurse and knew the factory in detail. She leaned over and whispered.

"You might be okay, but your son should get the injection. It's safer that way."

She handed me a prepared syringe containing a yellowish substance and an extra needle. I looked hesitantly at them. I took them despite being unsure whether to put them in my purse or not.

"I'll give you something to cover them with. I know it's outdated, but it's safer." She whispered softly.

She handed me a white handkerchief with darker stripes on its surface. I hadn't seen such a handkerchief in a long time. It was so similar to the one my grandmother used to carry in her purse. I burst into tears. Then I woke up.

Was it a message my grandmother's soul was trying to send me through that dream? Upon waking, I felt compelled to consider every possible superstition or spiritual explanation, as the dream had deeply affected me—I felt fear and confusion. When I saw the test results, the dream came back to me with striking clarity. What was I supposed to do?

Recently, I had been having strange dreams, finding myself in places that I remembered visiting in dreams before. Yet when I woke up, I realized I had never seen such places—and some of them didn't even exist in my waking life. Still, within the dream, they were so vivid and familiar. I told my mother about my dream with Denis, and she, attentive to our folk beliefs, remarked that a handkerchief symbolized tears.

I laughed then. I was tempted, as usual, to ignore such beliefs. However, after receiving my son's test results and because of the stress I was going through, I couldn't help but make a connection between the dream and results. Was this dream a premonition? Had something inside me sensed what was going to happen? Or was it just an unfortunate connection made by my mind as I attempted to find an answer to something which I couldn't explain logically?

Several months after the initial shock associated with discovering Denis's condition, the fear and concerns are still present. It turns out that Denis is at risk of developing diabetes—he has been diagnosed with pre-diabetes—which has completely changed our daily lives. What he eats, how much he eats, and when he eats are all things we have to consider every single day. As terrible as this news is, there is an added benefit to having this knowledge, too. I've learned that some of his emotional outbursts are linked to significant fluctuations in his blood sugar levels, whether too low or too high. And even though these moments often push me to the edge of my patience, I've come to understand that what Denis needs most is simply a lot of love.

It wasn't the first time I had seen something in a dream that later manifested in my life. However, in recent years, since I began my spiritual awakening, these phenomena have intensified. In January 2022, two weeks before the outbreak of the war in Ukraine, I experienced some strange and very clear dreams. In one, I saw soldiers marching through the city where I live, which had recently become an important NATO military center.

However, there was another dream that seemed much more coherent. It conveyed a clear message and influenced my understanding of recent events. In it, I saw a meadow where tanks, armored vehicles, and other military vehicles were advancing. Numerous soldiers carrying machine guns and other unfamiliar weapons marched past me, allowing me to see their facial expressions.

They were serious and focused. On their uniforms, I noticed the United States flag. In an instant, I understood that the USA was supporting a conflict, and what I was witnessing felt more like a metaphorical representation of broad support rather than direct involvement. How did I have this information? I can't explain it—I just knew it. From the way the soldiers moved, I sensed they weren't going to a training exercise but were preparing for a confrontation.

In the morning, I woke up in horror, gripped by the feeling that the extremely tense situation in Ukraine would soon develop into active hostilities. It was curious that I wasn't thinking of another war elsewhere in the world, but only of this potential conflict next to my country. While having breakfast, I told my mother about what I had dreamt. She was my first confidante, the one who listened to even my wildest thoughts and wouldn't judge me. I hadn't never experienced dreams like this before, and I was surprised by what was happening to me. My mother responded in a confident, categorical tone.

"Such a thing will never happen. Russia would never start a war against Ukraine. It doesn't make sense. What you saw were probably just military exercises."

I wasn't in a position to criticize her, but I felt there would be a conflict. The situation was almost comical. In my family, there's a mix of Ukrainian, Russian, Romanian, and Serbian blood. In this context, it was hard to even accept that such a conflict between Ukraine and Russia could happen. My feelings and beliefs were an inexplicable jumble of fear combined with the dreadful expectation that something really harmful was in store. Days passed, and I ignored the dream. On February 24, 2022, I was at the office when I received a notification on my phone saying that Russia had invaded Ukraine.

I was in shock the entire day. At the same time, I was glued by the news, following the rapidly unfolding events and trying to understand what was happening. I didn't know what frightened me more: the thought that I had anticipated these horrible events in a dream, suggesting that I might have the ability to foresee a catastrophe, or the horror and tragedy of the war itself, taking place just across the border from us in Romania.

It took me a long time to understand that premonition dreams should not be taken literally. For example, the dream in which I saw American soldiers marching through my city wasn't meant to be taken at face value. Instead, it symbolised their presence in my town because of the NATO centre that had recently been established. Rather than expecting events to unfold exactly as I had dreamt them, I came to realise that the message of the dream would manifest in a similar, but metaphorical, way. These are just two examples of dreams I had that alerted me to events that were about to happen—I had many more.

Why did this ability develop so late in my life, I wondered, and why did it happen to me? I had never believed in omens or dreams. But then again, I hadn't believed in many other extraordinary things either, yet I had experiences that completely changed my perspective. Through these experiences, and the knowledge I gained from them, I learned tolerance. I also learned to respect others' experiences, even if they seemed fantastical to me and hard to understand. After all, I reasoned, I wasn't the one experiencing them and couldn't judge their impact on someone else.

On the other hand, I realized that all the extraordinary metaphysical experiences I had seemed designed to push me out of my comfort zone and break down the logic-based barriers I had built over the years. I felt guided on this path and was convinced that all the new and previously unbelievable information was given to me in a way that I could internalize it without being overwhelmed.

Because of this awareness, I saw there was something I needed to learn by accessing this information about future events. And yet, I also knew I wasn't the only person who had premonition dreams. I reasoned there was most likely an explanation for why this ability had developed within me at this time. The one I offered myself was the possibility that I was accessing fragments of information from a collective consciousness that showed the most probable future scenario. This information was being given to me deliberately, but for what purpose? I had no way of knowing.

Towards the end of 2024, other events caught my attention, making me wonder if I was giving too much importance to every detail around me. In the past, I had ignored anything too exotic and focused on finding a quick and effective solution. Now, I was trying to find detailed explanations and paying more attention to my emotions and intuition. Because of my increased awareness and focus, I experienced some paranormal events in our home at the end of 2024. I had noticed strange things happening before, but this time the events occurred one after another and caught my attention.

In November, we were gathered in the living room. My son was watching TV, and my mother and I were discussing the preparations for the winter holidays, which lasted about a month due the individual saints' day, birthdays, Christmas, New Year's Eve, and Saint Nicholas Day. In the living room, behind the door, I kept a fabric box containing some children's books, including an instructional music book with a mini piano. From time to time, my son would choose a book for us to study together.

This time, my son was busy with his tablet, and I was in the middle of a conversation with my mother. Suddenly, I noticed musical sounds coming from the box filled with books stacked on top of each other, as if someone had pressed two keys. I looked around and checked the lamp to see if it was swaying. The sounds could have been triggered by an earthquake or a heavy truck passing by on the boulevard. My son hadn't moved from the armchair, and nothing in the house could have caused the books to move in any way. I concluded that the battery in the piano book was probably running low.

I continued my conversation with my mother, but after 15 seconds, I heard the sound again. This time, more than one key was pressed. I asked my mother, and she confirmed that she had heard it too. While we were talking, the music book sounded again. This time, I was sure something was in the room. So, in a confident voice, I spoke directly to whatever was in the other room.

"If you want to communicate, please use two sounds for yes, and one sound for no, okay?"

I could feel my adrenaline levels rising. I immediately heard two sounds. I had my confirmation, and I started asking questions.

"Are you here with us in the room?"

Again, two piano keys were touched.

"Are you someone we know? Do we know you?"

The answer was no.

"Are you alive?"

The answer was yes. Indeed, I perceived a column of gray smoke. It appeared to be a vaguely human figure, a male, standing by the door.

I continued, remaining alert.

"Do you want to communicate with me?"

No response came. I asked the question again, but still there was no answer. It seemed as if the male had figure disappeared. Strangely, my son didn't notice anything during this time. He would have been the first to react and ask what was happening. It was unusual. After five minutes, once I had recovered from the shock, I stood up and walked over to the box.

I could think of only one explanation. Perhaps the music book had been underneath other stacked books, and one of those on top had slipped, producing the sounds from the book below. It was unlikely, but I wanted to test it. When I lifted the lid, I saw that the piano book was on top of the stack, and the keys couldn't have been pressed in any way.

After that strange experience near the holidays in December, my mother reported feeling something touch her one evening. It was like a small tap on her cheek. It happened while we were at home and she was walking down the hallway from her bedroom to the living room. I started to feel suspicious again and I began to ask questions.

Could it be the same entity? Or was there more than one trying to communicate or play in a certain way? Were they trying to communicate with me or with my mom? Was there any link between the entities I communicated with during my astral journeys, or was it something else?

There were so many questions, and we had no real answers. But the strangest event happened one evening near Christmas. We were ready to sleep when, suddenly, the power went out, leaving us in the dark. The outage lasted for about half an hour. Later that night, we made sure that all the appliances we had plugged in were still functional. The TV remained on standby.

My mother turned on the TV to check if it was still working. She saw the button light up blue, indicating the device was on. Although it powered up, the screen remained black, and a message appeared, dancing on the screen: Samsung, Samsung. My mother checked the power button again. This time, it wasn't lit blue, indicating the TV was off. It seemed as if it hadn't been turned on. Yet, the message was large and clear on the screen: Samsung. The funny thing is, our TV is an LG. How was the TV showing us the message if it was turned off? There was no apparent explanation. My mother was deeply shocked. The recent events puzzled her even more. She was used to me having these types of experiences, but now that she was experiencing them herself, it was too much.

I didn't try to determine the reasons behind this series of phenomena because I couldn't find a logical explanation. They seemed to be a chain of almost successive events that appeared to be coincidences. Over the years, though, I learned that there are no coincidences. I felt these occurrences were signs, trying to convey something to me. Nothing scared me in these experiences, but I felt uncomfortable when I sensed the gray column of energy with a vague human shape in the room with us. I hesitated because I had learned to be cautious when detecting energy forms around me.

In the past, I learned a lesson on this subject. In 2007, I travelled alone to Tunisia and decided to tour a mansion-museum, Dar Essid, in the city of Sousse. During the visit, I entered the master's bedroom. One wall of the room was dominated by a sumptuous bed with a red cover and imposing, ostentatious curtains. From the moment I stepped into the large room, I was drawn to the bed's location; although, I couldn't pinpoint what attracted me to that spot.

I kept my eyes fixed on the bed, and the longer I stayed, the stronger the feeling grew that something terrible had happened there. It wasn't long before I was certain there had been a rape and murder in that room. While I stood there, alert to my senses, I felt a presence next to me, as if trying to drive me away. It was a male presence. In my mind, I felt compelled to speak up. A surge of rage coursed through me as the male energy grew stronger and more dominant, because at the same time, I could feel the horror and pain of the victim. I couldn't remain silent. In that moment, I felt an overwhelming need to seek justice for the victim and confront the killer.

"I know what you did."

From that moment, I felt a vibrational wave forming around me. I sensed the male energy directing a furious response at me. But I didn't leave. I communicated telepathically that I would go when I chose to—and not because he was driving me away, even though I understood it was his space. I confronted him openly. After a while, I decided to leave the room. I no longer felt safe. I was afraid for my life. As I left the bedroom and headed to the next room, I felt violently sick in an instant. I was directed to a restroom and spent half an hour there, actively vomiting and feeling sick to my stomach. I could barely stand.

With great difficulty, I went downstairs and, on my way out, I sought help from the women who worked as guides and security. I spoke to them in English, and they replied in French, but they could see that I was in a weakened and distressed state. They brought me a glass of water with sugar, and after another half hour, I recovered. I didn't continue my visit. After leaving the inner courtyard of the house and walking about 50 meters, I felt perfectly fine, as if nothing had happened. I tried to explain it to myself by considering the possibility of heatstroke, but no discomfort ever returned.

What I learned from this event is not to confront threatening spirits unless I have to and, above all, not to show fear in their presence. It wasn't the first time something like this had happened. I had similar experiences in Munich in 2005, where I sensed a presence in the corner of a room at Nymphenburg Palace, the main summer residence for the former rulers of Bavaria in the 17th and 18th centuries. Again, I could pinpoint the spirit's location and whether it was a male or female entity, but I couldn't describe its features.

As in Tunisia, I could also detect the entity's mood and the emotions it transmitted. There was sadness and shyness. This time I sensed a female shadow who was trying to hide. There was a feminine energy that seemed surprised and fearful of my ability to detect her. I was in one of the bedrooms, and the energetic presence was in the left corner. I felt that she had died there. It hadn't been a violent death, but rather one caused by illness. She was middle-aged but had a fragile presence. I decided not to disturb her. It was surprising that I could feel her presence—and even more so that she was aware of it too. It was as if we had met on the street, each of us in a different dimension, yet still able to sense one another.

As my curiosity grew, I decided to research the famous women who had died in Nymphenburg Palace. I discovered several, but one portrait particularly caught my attention— it was Princess Alexandra of Bavaria. She died aged 49 and was known to have delicate health, along with a number of psychological eccentricities, including a fixation on cleanliness as well as wearing only white clothes. There was something about her image that felt familiar to me, as if it resonated with the presence of the female entity I sensed in the palace. Could it have been her? I don't know the answer for certain—but somehow, I felt it was.

What I learned about myself through both experiences was that I was almost magnetically attracted to certain places, and I felt the need to connect with them through touch or a light meditative state. I was able to sense the energy of these places and even identify the presence of entities who wanted or didn't want to make their presence felt. Was I the one who wanted to contact them, or was it their way of drawing me into communication? I couldn't say. I also didn't understand how I could spot them regardless of their desire.

To be clear, I deliberately use the term "entity" instead of "ghost." I believe that the presences we sense, which try to get our attention in one way or another, are entities, not ghosts as commonly believed in folklore. My explanation for this is that, due to the vibrational level at which we operate, we can barely perceive an entity functioning on a different vibrational level with our physical and intuitive senses.

Certainly, our willingness to engage in such contact, as well as the extent to which we make use of the right hemisphere of our brain, associated with intuition, can enhance our ability to perceive these presences more easily. On the other hand, there also needs to be cooperation from the entity to reveal itself and make its presence felt. In this case, I would say that the entity adjusts its vibrational level to be compatible with the person it wants to contact. This could explain why, in some cases, I could feel the energetic presence, the emotions of the entity, and even provide some descriptive details.

This also begs the question: why do I refer to these beings as entities when, as in the events in Sousse and Munich, I sensed presences in places previously inhabited by people who died there? What I sensed might be just the presence of the people who died in those places, and not a separate entity that feels and acts on its own.

In this case, we might consider that we are not dealing with alive entities connected to that place but with possible energetic imprints of deceased individuals. Based on these questions, I considered three hypotheses.

My first hypothesis was that the soul, as an energetic body that detaches from the physical body upon death, maintains a connection with the place where the trauma of death occurred. Due to this trauma, it cannot detach from the place of death or the life it had, being unable to accept healing and reincarnate into another body. The energy of the soul is blocked in time and space until it decides to detach from that place and follow its path. There are guides waiting for the soul to decide to move to another plane of existence and resume the cycle of healing—choosing a new life lesson—in the form of reincarnation.

My second hypothesis is that certain places and objects retain an energetic imprint of their former owners, especially if the event that took place was extremely tragic or, on the contrary, extremely happy. This vibrational level, whether lower or higher than what we as humans usually operate at, is easy to detect in a mild state of meditation.

For example, there are places that seem to have no vibrational charge, but we feel that charge just by stepping into that place. We might be surprised by how a certain park or garden, which would normally energize us, drains our energy instead. Conversely, a simple painting can make us feel full of life and hope, transmitting something magical that is hard to describe in words. The energetic imprint can be preserved for years, regardless of whether the soul of the deceased is still in that place. In this second hypothesis, the objects and the place themselves retain a memory of that event, which can be revealed to an attentive person.

The third hypothesis is that places imprinted with tragic or joyful events can attract entities vibrating at the same frequency, potentially opening doors of communication or portals to other planes. It is difficult for me to say whether these planes have a higher or lower vibration, although it could be either. Such places may also attract manifestations into our existential plane. Entities using these forms of manifestation may have benevolent intentions or not. It is preferable to spend some time in their energy field to sense if their intentions are benevolent before initiating communication.

Depending on the situation and the mode of manifestation, I would consider all the above hypotheses and their applicability as possibilities. Based on the incidents I experienced at the end of 2024, I would lean more towards the third hypothesis. I certainly encountered a playful entity, whether it was joking or not. It is difficult to discern, but I clearly remember how they communicated their mood and emotions to me, and how this continued to affect me for days afterward.

Through these events, I realized that I possessed abilities that had been dormant within me and had now awakened, and I could not deny their existence after my experiences. I felt like a magnet attracting entities and extraordinary events, unable to control their occurrence or impact. Despite my desire for control, I realized their appearance was not about control but about learning to let go of control and allowing all these events to occur. In this way, a mutually beneficial relationship is formed, from which I could extract the greatest lessons.

I've come to several important conclusions from these experiences that I believe are of value to anyone who may be interested in exploring their own abilities. To start, I was surprised to learn that I could sense the presence of entities through the energetic imprint they leave behind. I can detect the exact location and the nature of the energy—whether it is benevolent or not, and whether it has a feminine or masculine presence—based on how the energy affects me. If I focus and close my eyes, I can even visualize physical details. To use this ability, I need to be alone, to concentrate, and to be in a quiet environment, free from loud noises or surrounding agitation.

Along with this, I discovered that despite the emotional impact an energetic presence may have on me, it is best not to confront it in any way. I learned I can refuse communication through carefully monitoring my thoughts and feelings, as these are often perceived by the energetical presence. However, I saw that provoking the presence can lead to consequences beyond my control. Just as I perceive the energetic imprint and try to understand more about the characteristics of the presence that wishes to communicate, that presence does the same with me. Any form of provocation can lead to an energetic imbalance, which may manifest as a loss of equilibrium, dizziness, stomach issues, or even fainting spells.

While some of them are reluctant, I've learned that most of these energetical presences try to communicate with me. It has been difficult for me to manage the heightened adrenaline these situations trigger and to approach them as something natural. Instead, I try to understand what they want to convey. Sometimes, they simply want to let me know they are there, and nothing more.

And I've learned to pay closer attention to the meaning of my dreams and to write down the ones that leave a strong impression on me. A helpful exercise for remembering details is to share the dream with someone right after waking and then write it down within a few hours. This practice helps imprint the dream more clearly in my memory, making it easier to recall later.

Finally, perhaps the biggest takeaway I have to offer is this: the world of dreams is closely aligned with our reality. It matters less whether we are tapping into a collective consciousness during sleep, catching glimpses of the future, or merely projecting our fears and hopes onto what lies ahead. What is within our reach is the ability to observe the dream world and extract lessons that are worth learning. The dreams that stir strong emotions in us often carry multiple layers of meaning—meanings that only we can interpret through the lens of our own experiences and the intuition we possess.

I also want to emphasize that it is very likely that presences exist around us, even when we are not aware of them.

Within the many dimensions and vibrational levels that make up our reality, there are energetic entities with which we occasionally come into contact. This happens either when they choose to reach out or when the barrier that separates us becomes thinner. Cultivating our intuition and paying close attention to our surroundings can enhance these forms of communication.

Chapter Fourteen

Bringing to a Boiling Point

I have lived my entire life on the edge. I saw myself as being on the edge of an abyss, waiting for something to happen, something to change and bring meaning to the day-to-day life I was living. As a child, I waited for my true life to appear. I felt it existed somewhere, and I wanted it to materialize so that I would no longer be forced to live a life I did not understand. During my youth, I ignored the intuition that always tried to warn me when I had made the wrong choice in a romantic relationship or a job, as I gave more importance to my mind and logic than to the heartfelt emotions screaming from within me. As an adult, I was again living on the edge between the logic dictated by my desire to adapt, to be like others, and the intuition that suggested there was much more to life than what I could measure with my mind and reason. It was a direction completely opposite to the one I had in childhood. Back then, I had chosen to seek and long for the unseen world. With age, I chose to ignore it entirely.

Despite all the experiences I had in childhood and youth, the year 2018 marked a true turning point in my life. Pregnancy, with all its heightened sensitivities, opened a door within me due to the fear I had of the possibility of having a child with medical issues. This door led me, step by step, to discovering myself through past lives, through exploring the Akashic realm and my Book, through astral journeys, through discussions with non-terrestrial entities, and a continuous telepathic connection with my partner, who holds dual roles as Xenex and Rico.

The process of learning more about this awakening process was mysterious as it revealed itself gradually. After visualizing several earthly lives, I began to connect with non-terrestrial lives through the Akasha. Yet, one of these lives I visualized played the role of a catalyst. It was a life in which the memories I had were related to the intention of incarnating on Earth alongside my partner, with a clear mission we had consciously undertaken: to study human emotions.

During one of my regressions in 2022, I experienced the process of transitioning from that non-terrestrial life into the body of a child born on Earth. The experience itself was frightening and weighed on me for a long time. Although it wasn't physically painful, I found it traumatic because I was unprepared for the transition from one existence to another and it caught me off guard. Even though I had agreed to this process, it occurred far too quickly and unexpectedly. The absence of mental preparation caused me to panic, and I felt with every fiber of my being how my energy was draining from my non-terrestrial entity's body into that of a newborn baby, spanning the two dimensions. For a short period, I existed in two different worlds and could be connected to both realms. In the end, I left the non-terrestrial plane behind and remained in the new world. This new terrestrial world scared me. I felt alone, and the excess of noise and colors were too much to bear. The spontaneous way in which the transition from one plane to another took place resulted in me leaving my partner on the other plane.

These insights I had in 2022, along with many others, contributed to my awakening to a new reality that differed significantly from what I encountered on social media or in my daily interactions. I was on this path in 2024, satisfied with the position I had reached and the new awareness that had taken place. Everything seemed to make sense, and I would gradually develop the ability to raise my vibration, detaching myself from the desire to control everything around me and redefining my perspectives on life. At the same time, I was able to be present in my reality and perfectly capable of trying to solve daily problems. The three-dimensional reality I lived as part of my daily life kept me well connected and did not allow me to internalize or completely detach.

Everything became complicated at the end of 2024 when, after some routine blood tests, I discovered that my little boy was suspected of having early-stage diabetes. Everything I had built within myself, that atmosphere of calm and serenity through my spiritual experiences, collapsed in an instant. The entire aura of spirituality that surrounded me like a cocoon unraveled in a few moments. I found myself once again as the same action-oriented, restless person, interested in the logic-based approach to the problem and how I could solve it. The need for control was reborn in me with unexpected force, and I was determined to transform myself into a Hercules to solve the problem my little boy might have, disregarding everything else around me.

With this pragmatism and a desire for action, I erased the unseen world in an instant. I didn't let my spiritual side speak, as I silenced it. Now, the warrior in me was needed, and the traveler between planes took a back seat. What activated the warrior within me was the fear that paralyzed me at that moment. I already realized that I was vibrating at a much lower frequency just through the feeling of fear that I couldn't quell.

I wasn't able to consider that perhaps all these suspicions of illness were meant as a life lesson for both me and my little boy, and that we had, most likely, chosen this life plan and this lesson together. Of course, I heard these thoughts somewhere in my mind, whispered by the inner voice of my intuition. But I ignored them and didn't want to accept that, as a soul, I could have agreed to such a plan. I had returned to square one, where I had started this journey in 2018. I was ignoring the voices within me.

I clung to a desire—the desire to be saved. I hadn't felt this urge since childhood and adolescence. I felt the need for support, a kind word, a miracle. I needed someone around me who was much stronger than I was, someone whose very presence could inspire this sense of security. Very rarely had I met someone stronger than myself. The lesson I had taught myself from youth until now was that I had to manage on my own, and therefore, I would never meet anyone who could offer me this comfort.

In that moment, I didn't need material or emotional support, I just wanted to feel that someone was more in control beside me when I felt the ground slipping from beneath my feet. Wasn't this also a lesson I needed to learn, to persevere on my own? Or was it simply a message that I didn't need control, but should relax and let things flow naturally? I even realized that when I forced things through my desire to control, I actually lost even more of it.

During those days, I refused to be contacted or to connect with other planes. I didn't feel capable of even attempting a connection, nor did I feel the desire to contact my partner in any of their known forms as Xenex or Rico. In the end, perhaps it was my mindset of self-sufficiency and independence that kept Rico's human form away. I now wonder if I could truly handle his masculinity and his constant need to protect me. Even if I had cried out for it, would I have been prepared? I perceived myself as a warrior, and despite my internal vulnerability, I was a master at hiding it.

I felt on the edge again. In my daily life, there were thousands of problems that needed solving. Being a single mother had taught me to be strong, but in my rush to do everything, I had lost my sensitivity and feminine elegance. I no longer had time to find myself and be alone with my thoughts. By the end of the year, exhaustion was overwhelming me, and it seemed like I couldn't find joy in anything I did. On the other hand, I remained focused on learning more about spirituality and wanted to continue on this path, feeding my curiosity.

Living on this edge between reality and dreams, between cold pragmatism and intuition, had defined me for a long time, but it was the first time I had gazed into the depths of the abyss created. Self-doubt dominated my thoughts. What was my path, and what was I supposed to do? How easy would it be to return to my spiritual side? If a significant event, such as my son's health, could derail me from the path I had chosen to integrate all that I had learned into my life, was I truly a spiritual person in this context? Or was I just mimicking this spirituality and awakening? Perhaps this spiritual awakening hadn't yet solidified within me, leaving me highly susceptible to reverting to my former self when faced with a disturbing event.

Coincidentally, the visions I used to have during lucid dreams or those at the border between sleep and wakefulness had become rarer. I would fall asleep easily before experiencing any kind of vision or sensations. There were nights when I had nightmares and woke up filled with anxiety. My presence in these realms that used to bring me peace in the latter part of the day had faded. Yet, I still had the same desire to learn more and seek answers in the Akasha, through astral journeys or discussions with the Lord of the Records. However, any presence I had in these spaces would quickly fade. The images became unclear; I lost focus and eventually fell asleep. My concentration was absent but centered on my daily experiences and worries. I didn't know how to regain my focus on the unseen world. I missed it.

After the shock I experienced with my son, and the need to accept the situation as it was—without being able to act or solve the problem as I was used to, I finally managed to balance my mental state, returning to a normal level of functioning and be a support for my son. I meditated a lot on the situation we were going through and my need to protect him more than ever. I remembered the regression from my past life and the difficulty with which I said goodbye to the fetus I hadn't given birth to, and how this concern had carried over the years and into this life.

I managed to accept that, perhaps, this trial we were both going through was connected to our roles in this life. My role was to guide him and teach him a different way of life by being attentive to a strict diet and loving him unconditionally. His role was to experience this way of life and carry it forward. As a mother, my role was to guide him as I had been guided many times by Xenex or the Lord of the Records, and as I had been warned by premonitions. I could only note that I was a receiver of messages from other planes that had the capacity to prepare, inform, guide, and warn me when necessary. I was not alone in my struggles in this life. Through premonitions or communication with other planes, I was constantly in contact with a part of myself that fueled me with the energy for the next day.

Deep down, I knew that despite the shock I had endured, the very arrival of my little boy had facilitated this awakening within me, which had been in a latent state, probably waiting to take shape at the right moment. Through these discoveries I made on this spiritual path, I realized how I could recreate my Self. I could transform into someone who believed without hesitation and, through this awakening, become more relaxed and tolerant—both towards myself and others. I would come to understand the life lesson for which I had chosen this body and this identity to return to this planet. However, in the meantime, everything around me had fallen apart, and I felt lost.

After simmering for a while, I decided to ask the Lord of the Records what was happening with me and my life, and why my access to other planes was being denied. I felt punished for not having such easy access anymore, even though I knew that in these spaces, there was only learning and no concept of punishment. I kept repeating to myself that something had happened. The Lord of the Records surprised me with his response.

"Your focus needs to be elsewhere. You are occupied with your second book, which is important not just for you... and I want you to have the necessary time in your world to give it the importance it deserves. Additionally, your life operates according to certain social conventions that have been extremely pressing lately. Moreover, you have decided to sleep with your son again, and his energy interferes with yours, reducing your level of concentration. Family life has absorbed you. You cannot exist in multiple places. For now, our discussions will take a back seat. But I can tell you that you will continue to write."

His communication was clear and focused on the words he was presenting, and it was rare for him to use this form of expression. What he was telling me seemed unacceptable. I needed that reality I lived in to sustain myself throughout the day as a hope for resurrection. So I pushed back.

"I need our discussions, I need Xenex's presence as my guide, I need everything that defines me with a past and a future, and I need astral journeys."

With a smile, he replied.

"But you do have them. I am with you, and we have discussions, but this time not about complex concepts that you would need to write about, because you don't have the time and energy to focus. Xenex is always with you, and sometimes you know you feel his presence and can visualize him. On the other hand, in the Akasha, the role of past lives is concluded, and you know the future scenario, so it's not necessarily important to know more now."

At that moment, I understood why I felt this blockage. It was coming from him, the Lord of the Records. Although I could no longer visualize him, I still felt his presence and heard him.

"You do not exist solely for this plane where the Akasha is, and you cannot be in contact only with this plane. You came into this body because you decided it was the best choice for your soul, and you need to live this life to the fullest. What you receive from us is to enrich you and remind you of where you come from and where you will return. You can even live without a continuous connection to this astral plane. Nothing has changed for you. You remain yourself. The same soul with the same capabilities."

The conversation resonated deeply within me. Once again, it was fear that made me cling to everything I had experienced over the past few years. It was the fear of loneliness, the fear that I wouldn't find any meaning in what I was doing or in living each day. Then I understood. All those hidden pieces of information and meanings I had been searching for, which had been in front of me all along, began to unlock within me.

I started to understand, step-by-step, that I was not just the sum of my experiences in this life, but within me were fragments from many other lives. There were fragments from the inflexible and cold priestess who wanted to unite tribes, and from the noble Greek woman married to a Roman who knew the fear of Nero's dungeons. I also knew the disdain of people from my life as a prostitute and what it meant to end up hanged for this sin. All those experiences—fears, disappointments, pains, longings, passions, and, not least, love—still lingered within me.

And yes, I missed those I had parted with in all those lives. I realized that within me there were also fragments of future lives and what I was to become as I detached from this place. All these constituted parts of me, even if I was not in constant contact with other non-terrestrial beings and did not receive as much information as I would have liked or wanted, and even if there was no sustained telepathic communication with Xenex or Rico.

I realized once again that what we call time in our conventional human system did not exist. Time did not exist as a continuous, relentless, linear flow, and therefore you were not captive of everything that had happened to you in the past, trying to redeem your mistakes. All these mistakes and life scenarios were lived anyway in the form of alternative timelines in a variety of parallel worlds.

On the other hand, if I considered the concept as presented to me by the Lord of the Records, parallel universes could be defined and rearranged. The realities of experienced events were redefined through the lens of the present, and the past and future could be rearranged in a completely different form. In the end, this sophisticated concept of parallel universes was just a mirage, a holographic reality created for a soul to experience change and the desire to manifest externally. And above all, this mechanism was the Source itself, as the supreme and unique consciousness, wanting to test its limits and representing the final point, the beginning, and the end.

What I hadn't understood before was that there was no concept of becoming a spiritual being. Each of us was spiritual in one form or another. This part was well hidden within us, waiting to be activated at a certain moment. Being spiritual didn't grant me or anyone any special quality or the right to judge those around me who might not share my beliefs. However, I was responsible for sharing my experiences. Living these extraordinary experiences didn't mean that I would quickly transform from a pragmatic and logical person into a balanced, Zen-like individual, similar to Buddhist monks who could maintain their serenity in the face of any change and transcend it effortlessly.

I was who I was. I was subject to extremes, and this was likely the way I was meant to function in this life. I could learn to be more tolerant, but I still reacted firmly to acts of injustice, feeling indignation and wanting to respond assertively. I still wanted to choose and control the path I had to follow in this life, even though there were more and more moments when I could surrender to the present and find my inner peace. I was a warrior type, having seen and understood my path from my last non-terrestrial life. This warrior spirit was activated in this human life more than I expected, and I couldn't help it. I didn't feel as if I was special, and I would be open to listening—and, above all, resist the urge to advise or change others when it wasn't my place.

As I have reached this moment in my life, I realize my soul plan could be different from what I originally thought. I see now that the goal isn't to lose my human qualities and flaws but to learn from them. I am meant to try to shape myself based on the knowledge and skills I have acquired and used to develop myself. I feel that, gradually, my position on the edge of the abyss has changed. I am returning to a normalcy between the two planes of reality I experience. And I see that the abyss is no longer there. Instead, it is filled with pieces of me, each one representing a new facet of myself.

Chapter Fifteen

Conclusion

As I complete my book, I would like to highlight what I believe are the most important themes from *On the Edge*.

The first thing I want to emphasize is that everything we consider final, certain, and stable, like the laws of physics, is relative and subject to change faster than we can anticipate. Change occurs in the events we experience and at an individual level. It also is present in the reality-based life we lead every day and how the universe operates, which are in constant flux. This requires us to adapt to changing circumstances and assimilate new information.

Among the conditions I am learning to live with is the importance of being flexible and open to new experiences. This includes embracing new ideas and perspectives, intriguing information, and anything that challenges the comfort zone of my thinking and way of life. Naturally, there are many moments when this influx of new information is hard to assimilate, analyze, and accept. Even so, I continue practising conscious openness to expand my understanding. The ultimate goal is not necessarily to validate others' perceptions and feelings but to broaden my own perspective.

Another behavior I have adopted is not judging others. Given our experiences and the tendency to draw parallels between what we know and what others know, we often categorize things as good or bad. I practice not judging and instead ask additional questions to understand the reasoning and emotions behind someone's perspective, which often brings me new information. I relax and listen to other people as they express their thoughts, and I am often surprised by how different our experiences can be, yet we can still find common ground. This non-judgmental approach has brought me significant benefits not only personally but also in business. Additionally, it has relieved me of the burden of advising and counseling others when it is not requested.

I have also learned to love with every fiber of my soul. This certainly applies to the beautiful images of past lives, my beloved past partner in his present form with everything he represents, my wonderful guide, and any information that satisfies my curious nature. It also applies to the thousands of small aspects I experience daily: a lunch with colleagues, my son mispronouncing "high school" as "toilet school," being late to an important meeting, and the small details we often overlook in search of the significant ones. I have discovered within myself infinite resources to love everything around me, as well as myself, with all my physical and emotional imperfections.

I am still learning to accept that others are just a continuation of me and a reflection in the mirror, whether it's a driver who cuts me off or a bad experience in a mall. Even though I understand my role in this intellectually, I am not yet sure that I truly feel it deep inside as I do when I am in the astral realm.

I have learned to accept what happens to me and not to try to control the visions or where they lead, even though I still don't have a clear certainty about the future steps I must take or what lies ahead. Yet, I feel that that the magic lies in not being surprised by what happens to me. This duality still persists—between my pragmatic daily life and my astral, spiritual existence. My communications with non-terrestrial beings are present on various levels, all with the same encouragement to speak openly about them, because this information doesn't belong to me; it belongs to everyone. The end result is that I embrace this role with enthusiasm, as I am pleased to share it with you.

The experiences may seem disconnected from one another, making them appear less credible. Additionally, it might be hard to comprehend this continuous dual existence I lived as I tried to integrate it harmoniously with my earthly reality.

On the other hand, I wanted to share my life story on this path of self-transformation and try to identify when the first signs of this spiritual awakening appeared. For me, it was crucial to create this path and connect the transition points from one experience to another to gain an overall understanding of my state. This tumultuous period of experiences and manifestations made much more sense and had a greater impact on me after I learned to highlight important references from the communications as guidance and warnings.

Another aspect I want to highlight is the emotional experiences I had and how they affected me. I can say that the emotional rollercoaster was intense each time, during and after such manifestations, and it was difficult to sustain, especially in the early part of this spiritual journey. I tried to deny and reject many of the visualizations and manifestations that appeared around me in various forms, while my logical side feverishly sought a way to contain and label what was happening so I could achieve emotional calm.

I gradually regained my calm when I allowed my intuition to manifest more frequently and guide the process, even in the absence of logical and tangible evidence as my mind demanded. Without understanding the emotional impact created by all these manifestations, simple visualizations might be viewed from a purely pragmatic and logical perspective, analyzed only against a backdrop of dry and rigorous data. However, each piece of information is imbued with an emotional imprint for both the receiver and the sender.

I understood that I needed to change my approach for my own well-being. I had to let go of control. I stopped trying to control or influence these communications according to my desires—whether I wanted them or not, in the way I preferred, and particularly with the beings I chose. By surrendering control to the universe, I managed to relax and enjoy this journey, wherever it led me.

I also came to understand that my urge to control was driven by a fear of losing the manifestations I had grown used to. It was my little private corner where I could retreat from what was happening in reality. It took some time for me to realize that these manifestations were a form of escaping from myself, highlighting my insecurities about my own abilities, the channels I had developed, and the lack of trust I had in the entities I was connected with. Additionally, my exaggerated control indicated that, besides my fluctuating self-esteem, I also identified a low level of self-love. I didn't respect myself in this relationship and, as a result, I exhausted myself in the search to validate and revalidate what I was experiencing. I believe this was one of the most important life lessons I received from them indirectly.

I invested time and energy in validating the information received from past terrestrial lives, especially in the case of the first life I visualized. However, I now consider that I invested too much energy in a closed past, trying to bring to light as much information and dormant emotions as I could. The abyss of emotions I plunged into was dizzying, and I had difficulties drawing demarcation lines between past and present, and detaching myself from what I had been and what I had loved. On the other hand, these actions also brought positive aspects, helping to heal wounds that were still festering and in need of soothing.

I have no regrets about any of these past actions, which I now see in a completely different light. They had their purpose, and I learned from them, bringing me to where I am today. However, for the future, I would like to continue on this path, fully enjoying these experiences and the way they will shape me as a person and in terms of my consciousness. Despite my connections with non-terrestrial entities, I feel more grounded than ever and deeply tied to this place where I have spent many lifetimes, regardless of what my next step as a soul will be.

As for you, my reader, I invite you to carry with you a few inspirational thoughts—ideas to reflect upon and explore for yourself:

- Nothing in life is final; certain experiences open

new doors and invite us to journey through different realms.

- We are more than just this one life on Earth. Our souls are eternal, carrying fragments of many lives and experiences as we travel as energetic beings through the universe.

- We are guided on our path of spiritual awakening—even if that guidance comes only as a whisper or a déjà vu.

- We are capable of perceiving hidden realms, as long as we remain open and non-judgmental about what we receive as messages.

- Ultimately, we are the key to our own transformation, in whatever direction we choose to go.

I will conclude this book about my spiritual awakening with a final discussion I had with the Lord of Records about human nature and life on Earth.

One morning before Christmas 2024, while dropping off my little boy at kindergarten—dropping him off meant more like stopping the car in front of the kindergarten until he could get out and then rushing off to work—I signaled left to enter the main road. It was 8:00 AM, and the road was, as usual, very busy. There were lines of cars heading towards the industrial area where most of the city's companies were located. Even though it would have been obvious that I had just dropped off my son and wanted to rejoin the traffic, two cars passed by me, with the drivers completely ignoring me. I noticed through the window that the drivers were women, around my age. However, the third car, driven by a man, gave me the right of way, allowing me to join the line.

Back in traffic, I thought about what had happened. I knew it wasn't the first time. Why do women tend not to give way in traffic? I was a mother, and they probably were too, considering their age. Surely, they understood the morning madness of getting the little ones ready and rushing them to various places. They should understood these things much more than men, who in my country tend to be much more traditional and even rough. Shouldn't there be solidarity in this case, of mutual support among women? Why would a man be more considerate in this case? I didn't think it was just gentlemanly etiquette that made most men give way.

Suddenly, I heard a voice in my ear: "Survival. The instinct of survival."

I instantly recognize the presence—it was the Lord of Records. I was thrilled to sense him again. His appearances had become rare, and we no longer shared the long conversations we once had.

"You've come," I said telepathically. I knew he wanted to talk. His unexpected appearance and the fact that he jumped straight into the topic without any introduction made it clear. He got straight to the point.

"It is the survival instinct that dictates at this moment, and it is even more present in women than in men. Because they protect the family. When a woman feels threatened or is under stress, the survival instinct will emerge. Then she will disregard everything and everyone, focusing solely on protecting her family. In your case today, you can observe how many women are stressed and disconnected from the community. Men also react to stress by activating their survival instinct, but they have the capacity to be more empathetic towards those they consider more fragile than themselves and to feel a need to protect them."

Although the topic interested me, I was simply delighted to talk with him again about anything, just for the sake of talking. I had missed his presence. I asked him another question.

"So, which part is stronger in a person? Their survival instinct dictated by their organic side, or the matrix particle that composes the soul and carries the imprint of love specific to the Source?"

The response comes to me quickly.

"This is the interesting point: human behavior is divided into two main types of reactions during their lives on Earth. One is based on love, stemming from the material that makes up the soul, the matrix particle that forms all energy. The other is based on fear, emitting low-frequency vibrations due to the way human DNA is created. The human survival instinct is found in emotions like fear, frustration, despair, and anger, and most souls predominantly react to these. This causes souls incarnating on Earth to experience a constant duality in this holographic life. Many souls get lost in living this human life, operating solely on the survival instinct dictated by their organic nature, and forgetting where they came from. Many souls on Earth are young souls and fall into this trap, keeping their vibration low and preventing their vibrational level from rising."

I was familiar with the concept of young souls, but I wanted to clarify what he meant by this.

"When you refer to young souls, what exactly do you mean?"

"Young souls don't mean that these souls lack millions of years of experience in the universe or that they don't have a high level of consciousness. I call these souls young as they haven't experienced a physical body. Earth is different and challenging due to this created duality. It's an experimental world that has sparked the desire of many souls to experience something new and unique. Thus, many souls without any bodily experience decided to come to Earth to accelerate their evolution. They were convinced they could bring all the accumulated light and wisdom from higher planes, but they couldn't. The low vibration of Earth and lack of experience with such worlds combined with the forgetting they experienced caused them to get lost, and their evolution didn't happen as they had hoped. Their goal was to raise Earth's vibration in a much shorter time, but it didn't happen. Now, souls with experience in harsher worlds are needed to help with ascension through incarnation. Warrior souls as I call them. However, this word doesn't have negative connotations. For us, warriors are souls who are comfortable with changes, thrive in hostile environments and can adapt to them." The communication faded.

I pondered our discussion for many days. Was Earth's environment so corrupted and burdensome that raising one's vibration through a change in attitude, perception, and conception had become so difficult? Were we so entrenched in our automatic way of being and living, with such a limited range of abilities, that we couldn't rise above our level of consciousness as busy individuals, parents, colleagues, children, offering only detachment and indifference to those outside our intimate circle? Was this truly the essence of Earth that we were meant to learn through our incarnation here on our planet?

I received the answer during another conversation with the Lord of Records at the beginning of 2024, while driving to work and feeling an intense longing for myself and my partner Rico, and the absurdity of the situation I felt I was in. I heard him whisper.

"It's fascinating how the human race, due to its body, can generate so many negative thoughts and emotions. You are now trapped by these emotions, and your very DNA feeds on them. Negative emotions produce a substance in your body that acts like a drug, making your body crave more of it and amplifies these negative emotions. The mind follows suit, replaying catastrophic thoughts repeatedly to ensure the necessary amount of this substance is produced. This is actually a defense mechanism of the physical body and a way to compensate for the low-frequency level of Earth. The stronger this state of enslavement to negative emotions, the clearer the 3D reality experienced on Earth becomes, integrating the person more easily.

In individuals where the soul takes the initiative and counters the body's need for the addictive substance that keeps it at a low vibrational level, the soul will manage to integrate the person at a higher vibrational level but also cause a certain detachment from the 3D reality, leading to a sense of disconnection and loneliness. This is exactly what you are feeling now. Additionally, in your case, this most challenging incarnation you are going through is also your last. All the negativity and trauma experienced need to be released from both of you. You don't face many physical trials; they are mostly psychological. You need to relearn who you are, accept, and perhaps confront the emotion you haven't faced in other earthly lives—longing. Longing for each other, longing for home."

I knew then that the "home" he referred to was not a planet or a specific place, but the soul's longing to be free and to integrate into the absolute. My home is the universe.

Chapter Sixteen

Appendix: Questions and Answers

As I wrap up my book, I would like to first answer some questions that arose after the publication of my second book *(Conversation with Xenex)*, and during the process of writing *On the Edge*. Many readers may have similar questions. By answering them in this appendix, I hope to clarify some potential issues.

After the release of *Conversation with Xenex*, I received criticism from someone who, after reading the book's description, suggested that it was arrogant of me to think that all this information about the universe was given only to me by non-terrestrial entities. They indicated that it would have been more credible if this information had been addressed to everyone and not just a select few. Despite the cynicism with which it was conveyed, I found their perspective interesting and challenging, and I would like to address these concerns that others might also have.

From my experience with communicating with non-terrestrial entities, they choose the right moment to present themselves and, more importantly, to whom. One possible reason for their selectivity is the openness of the person to new experiences and their ability to engage in such communications. In other situations, and for other non-terrestrial races, the reason for contact may lie in the role the person holds and their power to effect change. In my case, my initial communication was exclusively with Xenex, in his role as a guide and partner. Later, through him, I was introduced to other entities, which I perceived positively due to his presence nearby. Another group of entities I met through Rico, Xenex's human form, as they were somehow connected to him. Eventually, their contact with me became separate from Xenex's presence.

I now understand that all these steps were chosen to familiarize me with them and their nature, giving me time to get used to telepathic communication and to understand the messages they had to convey. I perceived their appearances as always accompanied by a clear personal agenda, which, once achieved, allowed the communication to conclude successfully. In these interactions, I felt that it wasn't just me testing the communication channel, but they were doing the same. The more resistant I was to these communications, the less frequent the manifestations became. They would reappear, but they gave me time to process and to welcome them with a more open attitude. My free will in deciding whether or not to communicate with them was always respected. Refusing communication was equivalent to closing it. I am convinced that if they had encountered someone who firmly refused any type of communication from the start, this free will would have been respected.

There is another aspect to mention in addition to the above. The way, time, and form in which a communication channel develops over time for a person to receive this information also depends on the degree of our own consciousness development. Some people experience communications with deceased family members, others are guided by angels, and some receive messages from non-terrestrial entities. From my experience, the transmitter of the message and the type of communication channel matter only to the receiver, the person to whom the message is intended. What is critical, however, is the information itself, not just for the recipient but also for those around who wish to receive it.

From another perspective, each of us, as human and spiritual beings, is on a path of self-discovery, an intimate and specialized journey based on each person's needs. Each person's awakening occurs at the right moment and usually under unforeseen circumstances. The additional information we receive comes only when our consciousness is prepared to handle it so that we will be disturbed just enough to lead to growth and development of consciousness. It is all part of a long-term, step-by-step process. This was also the case for me.

I am convinced that many people are in this process of awakening and have experiences that cannot be explained. But how many people acknowledge to themselves that they are going through something extraordinary? How many of them will have the courage to confide in those close to them? And how many will take on the responsibility to speak out and share their experiences? From what I've seen, very few.

In conclusion, I don't believe I am the only one who has received information through extraordinary experiences, but I am among the few who have chosen to speak openly about it. I don't claim credit for this choice, as I have always felt an inner compulsion—supported by those around me—to share it. The wisdom of this decision to express myself was ultimately solidified through my communications with the Lord of the Records. This urge to write and share was given to me primarily to work on my own level of consciousness and to learn not to fear potential criticism because I shared information that could impact others who are seeking it.

The ultimate goal is to increase confidence in what we represent for ourselves and the universe, recognizing that we are all part of creation and creation itself. I am convinced that you will find ideas in the book that have resonated with you in the past. The same concept can be perceived from multiple perspectives depending on the observer, but the essence remains the same. The core is common, and different perspectives ultimately converge towards the same core. It is like children's drawings that are created from dots that they connect to form an overall picture. Similarly, I believe there are people who, like me, describe extraordinary experiences. Each of us is like a dot that, when connected with others, creates a comprehensive picture of a concept.

Finally, I would like to address some of the questions that have been raised about the topics addressed in this material.

Q: You test and name various methods through which you manage to travel with an astral body, access past lives, and even connect with entities like the Lord of the Records. Is it possible for you to provide clearer steps that can be duplicated and applied?

A: Indeed, I found it interesting to mention all the unconventional approaches I took in my quest to satisfy my curiosity and enhance these communications with various planes. However, this book is not intended to detail these methods, which I have validated solely through personal application, not through third parties. These descriptions of my methods represent just a fragment of my attempts to find the most suitable channels for me in these astral journeys, and thus, I cannot say whether replicating them will work universally for others. The reason is that each person has their own specific lessons to learn. If, in my case, the gateway for these lessons was the memories of past lives and accessing them through the Akashic realm, for another person, something entirely different might work. For me, accessing the Akashic realm was the easiest way to explore other realms and later develop my own methods to access new planes.

On the other hand, I did not conceive this book as a guide to be followed and replicated, nor have I considered, at least for now, developing such a guide. What I can say, however, is that any method tested individually and producing the desired results without endangering the person's mental and physical integrity could be considered. Group or individual methods can be taken into account. To enhance access to information, someone who values interaction with others might explore regression hypnosis sessions with specialists, engage in healing-based therapies, practise yoga, meditate, join spiritual discussion groups, or experience various shamanic ceremonies. A person who prefers the intimacy of their home and enhancing their own abilities by analyzing their experiences and states might use reading and journaling to note observations about what they experience.

What is truly important in this entire process of analysis is the person's presence in the present moment by observing their own states. Increasing focus on what is felt, seen, observed, and experienced can naturally lead to noticing signs of extraordinary experiences more easily. This process also requires testing one's patience and allowing the relinquishment of control to let events unfold naturally.

Q: After all the information you've received from these discussions with various entities, what question would you ask the universe based on everything you've learned?

A: This is by far one of the most challenging questions I've received from a reader, as there are so many questions I would ask, and certainly a limited number of answers I would receive, considering the limitations of my understanding as a human being and the level of consciousness at which I currently operate. From my experience in communications, especially with the Lord of the Records, after the initial surge of my questions and requests for clarification, I often found myself at a mental block. I was so overwhelmed by the details and the topic itself that I couldn't think of new questions to ask. They simply vanished from my mind easily. On the other hand, I would become mentally exhausted and feel the need to withdraw from the conversation, sit down, and transcribe what had been conveyed to me as soon as possible. Sustaining such communication over a longer term seemed difficult.

In this case, I believe I would modestly reconsider what I could ask the universe to show and explain to me. Most likely, I would wish to receive information that I could grasp with my human understanding and internalize so that I could extract the maximum lessons from it. Considering the mental blocks, I might develop and how I would like them addressed, I would prefer to receive answers to my questions in a visual-conceptual manner rather than acoustically, as the complexity of the information is too difficult to convey solely through language.

Ultimately, the question I would ask would be: "If there is an end to a soul's journey, what does it look like? Is there a finality to this journey, or is it an infinite cycle of energy remodeling without an end?"

It's interesting that after asking myself this question, I felt within me the corresponding answer received during conversations with Xenex and the Lord of the Records. I will try to summarize the ideas they presented.

The Source represents perfection itself, symbolized by a circle with a dot inside. The Source is both the dot and the circle at the same time. On one hand, the Source represents the inner dot when it is in a state of non-manifestation, in singularity and perfection. On the other hand, the Source represents the circle when, through its desire to manifest, it sends fractions of its energy outward, thus becoming a collective of Sources and losing its singularity.

The Source desires this manifestation out of a need to self-experience, to learn new things about itself, and for the sake of enjoyment. During these periods of manifestation, the Source releases fractions of its energy, from which souls are formed. These souls will experience various forms of manifestation and multiple realities to gain this form of learning and develop themselves. This cycle can be infinite until the Source decides to re-enter the cycle of non-manifestation, and all these souls reintegrate into the Source along with the accumulated knowledge.

Upon the return of the soul's energy to the Source, it becomes denser and enters the cycle of non-manifestation. The souls that integrate into the Source do not "find their death" but become part of the Source, without perceiving their individuality as strongly as when they had an individual form. They will be part of the collective consciousness of the Source. These cycles will repeat infinitely. In conclusion, there is no end of the road, only continuous transformation.

Q: You talk about the existence of Rico in the present life, incarnated, and with whom you have telepathic communications. Aren't you interested in whether he really exists and, if he does, in taking practical steps to meet him?

A: I firmly believe that Rico is real and has his own life somewhere in this world, just as I do. I've received numerous personal details from him that have allowed me to reconstruct periods of his life, learn about his passions, occupation, secrets, personality, and how he acts in this life. The experiences and images are too vivid to question their authenticity. Additionally, there have been confirmations regarding the information received from him, which I could partially verify. Therefore, he is as real to me as any other person in my life.

Based on the information I had, I undertook searches to confirm his identity. However, I never had clear information about his name, which is crucial when trying to find someone or a clear address. There were times when our telepathic communication was solely based on the desire to meet and remove any barriers we perceived between us. We had moments of intense turmoil, where we released all the negative emotions we had accumulated and the frustration of not being able to make this meeting happen practically. We rebelled against the universe, our guides, and the absurdity of our situation, seeking explanations in the Akashic records or from the universe. The constant advice we received was to be patient and focus on our spiritual paths, which involved missions both separately and together.

Over time, our determination softened, and we accepted each other with all these uncertainties and what was happening to us. No matter how much we tried to force this meeting through logical, human planning, it never materialized. The frustration intensified when we could sense each other's energy so vividly that it felt almost tangible, yet an invisible barrier seemed to keep us apart.

In the end, we accepted that it was beyond our power to change these aspects and that there was a universal order that surpassed us that we couldn't understand. There was an alignment between what we represented, our relationship to the life plan we existed in, and the entire universe. There were no exit door or shortcuts we could access to force that moment. It was just the right moment when everything could align.

Q: I found it really difficult to accept and integrate the chapter "Being a Ball of Light." It wasn't that I didn't understand it, but I struggled to relate to the subject. Why do you think some of your readers might have a hard time empathizing with this part?

A: I understand that some chapters might be difficult to relate to. As humans, it's challenging to empathize with experiences we haven't personally encountered. Even if we grasp the concept intellectually, truly accepting it requires our emotions and core values to align with the subject. That's the hardest part.

We are accustomed to relying on our five senses to test and prove things. When we lack this ability, we tend to deny experiences that fall outside our daily understanding. How did we get here? As children, we were inclined to believe in mysteries and extraordinary phenomena. However, as we grow, our global society teaches us that anything unusual must either be tested or denied and is often categorized as an illness. We've lost our capacity to believe without proof. Even religion, which asks for faith without proof, is often neglected due to the same inability to provide evidence.

Anything that falls outside our normal world makes us feel uneasy and unable to accept or believe it. Our Earth has functioned based on these norms for centuries. The only people who tend to be believers are those who have experienced something extraordinary themselves. They are more open to hearing from others who have gone through similar inexplicable states of mind.

Printed in Dunstable, United Kingdom